First World War
and Army of Occupation
War Diary
France, Belgium and Germany

38 DIVISION
115 Infantry Brigade
Welsh Regiment
16th Battalion
4 December 1915 - 27 February 1918

WO95/2561/3

The Naval & Military Press Ltd
www.nmarchive.com
Published in association with The National Archives

Published by

The Naval & Military Press Ltd

Unit 10 Ridgewood Industrial Park,

Uckfield, East Sussex,

TN22 5QE England

Tel: +44 (0) 1825 749494

www.naval-military-press.com

www.nmarchive.com

This diary has been reprinted in facsimile from the original. Any imperfections are inevitably reproduced and the quality may fall short of modern type and cartographic standards.

© Crown Copyright
Images reproduced by permission of The National Archives, London, England, 2015.

Contents

Document type	Place/Title	Date From	Date To
Heading	WO95/2561/3 16 Battalion Welsh Regiment		
War Diary	38th Division 115th Infy Bde 16th Bn Welch Regt Dec 1915-Feb 1918		
War Diary	16th Welsh Rgt. Vol 1 121/7910 38th Dis		
War Diary	Hazeley Down Winchester	04/12/1915	04/12/1915
War Diary	Southampton Havre	05/12/1915	05/12/1915
War Diary	St. Quentin	06/12/1915	20/12/1915
War Diary	Robecq	21/12/1915	29/12/1915
War Diary	St. Vaast	30/12/1915	31/12/1915
Heading	16th R Welsh Rgt Vol 2		
War Diary	St. Vaast	01/01/1916	06/01/1916
War Diary	Robecq	07/01/1916	14/01/1916
War Diary	Robecq Riez Bailleul	16/01/1916	22/01/1916
War Diary	Riez Bailleul Croix Marmuse	23/01/1916	31/01/1916
Heading	16th Welsh Rgt Vol 3		
War Diary	Reference Map 36 W. 3	01/02/1916	04/02/1916
War Diary	Croix Barbee	05/02/1916	15/02/1916
War Diary	La Pannerie	16/02/1916	17/02/1916
War Diary	Locon	17/02/1916	23/02/1916
War Diary	Festubert	24/02/1916	29/02/1916
Heading	H Welsh Reg Vol 4		
War Diary	Festubert	01/03/1916	16/03/1916
War Diary	Les Choqeaux	17/03/1916	24/03/1916
War Diary	Gorre	25/03/1916	27/03/1916
War Diary	Givenchy Lez La. Bassee	28/03/1916	31/03/1916
War Diary	Givenchy Lez La. Bassee	01/04/1916	09/04/1916
War Diary	Les Choquaux	10/04/1916	13/04/1916
War Diary	Neuf Berquin Estaires	14/04/1916	15/04/1916
War Diary	Laventie	16/04/1916	30/04/1916
War Diary	La Gorque	01/05/1916	08/05/1916
War Diary	Riez Bailleul	09/05/1916	09/05/1916
War Diary	Moated Grange Sector	13/05/1916	17/05/1916
War Diary	Riez Bailleul	18/05/1916	21/05/1916
War Diary	Moated Grange Sector	22/05/1916	22/05/1916
War Diary	Grange Sector	23/05/1916	25/05/1916
War Diary	La Gorgue	01/06/1916	04/06/1916
War Diary	Laventie	05/06/1916	10/06/1916
War Diary	La Gorgue	10/06/1916	11/06/1916
War Diary	Robecq	11/06/1916	13/06/1916
War Diary	Auchel	14/06/1916	14/06/1916
War Diary	Monchy Breton	15/06/1916	26/06/1916
War Diary	Fortel	27/06/1916	27/06/1916
War Diary	Autheux	28/06/1916	29/06/1916
War Diary	Toutencourt	30/06/1916	30/06/1916
Heading	War Diary 16th Battn. The Welch Regiment. July 1916		
War Diary	Toutencourt	01/07/1916	02/07/1916
War Diary	Acheux	02/07/1916	03/07/1916
War Diary	Buire S/L'Ancre	03/07/1916	04/07/1916
War Diary	Carnoy	05/07/1916	12/07/1916
War Diary	Warloy	13/07/1916	13/07/1916

War Diary	Couin	14/07/1916	14/07/1916
War Diary	Hebuterne Sectn	14/07/1916	18/07/1916
War Diary	Courcelles	19/07/1916	21/07/1916
War Diary	Hebuterne Sect.	22/07/1916	26/07/1916
War Diary	Courcelles	26/07/1916	27/07/1916
War Diary	Vauchelles	28/07/1916	30/07/1916
War Diary	Candas	30/07/1916	30/07/1916
War Diary	St Omer Millam	31/07/1916	31/07/1916
War Diary	Millam	01/08/1916	03/08/1916
War Diary	Merckeghem	03/08/1916	19/08/1916
War Diary	Poperinghe.	19/08/1916	19/08/1916
War Diary	Ypres	19/08/1916	31/08/1916
Miscellaneous	To 115 Inf Bde.		
War Diary	B.H.Q. Machine Gun F2	01/09/1916	05/09/1916
War Diary	Bn. H.Q. Chateau des 3 Tours	06/09/1916	06/09/1916
War Diary	B.H.Q. Canal Bk	10/09/1916	14/09/1916
War Diary	B.H.Q. Canal Bk Chat Des 3 Tours	14/09/1916	16/09/1916
War Diary	Camp P	16/09/1916	25/09/1916
War Diary	Bn H. Qrs Camp P	26/09/1916	30/09/1916
War Diary	Camp P	01/10/1916	02/10/1916
War Diary	Machine Gun Fm	03/10/1916	03/10/1916
War Diary	H.Q. Machine Gun Farm	08/10/1916	14/10/1916
War Diary	Chateau Des Trois Tours	15/10/1916	29/10/1916
War Diary	Camp E	30/10/1916	31/10/1916
War Diary	Camp E	01/11/1916	04/11/1916
War Diary	Canal Bank	04/11/1916	08/11/1916
War Diary	Turco	09/11/1916	14/11/1916
War Diary	Turco Trois Tours Chau	15/11/1916	18/11/1916
War Diary	Lancs Farm	19/11/1916	25/11/1916
War Diary	Camp P	26/11/1916	30/11/1916
War Diary	Camp P	01/12/1916	03/12/1916
War Diary	Left Support Bn. Right Bde (Turco)	04/12/1916	08/12/1916
War Diary	Support Bn. Turco Secn	09/12/1916	11/12/1916
War Diary	Boesinghe Front Line	12/12/1916	14/12/1916
War Diary	Boesinghe	14/12/1916	17/12/1916
War Diary	L Line	17/12/1916	31/12/1916
War Diary	Merckeghem	31/12/1916	13/01/1917
War Diary	Merckeghem	13/01/1917	13/01/1917
War Diary	Camp P	14/01/1917	14/01/1917
War Diary	Roussel Fm	15/01/1917	15/01/1917
War Diary	Boesinghe	16/01/1917	20/01/1917
War Diary	Bleuet Fm	21/01/1917	24/01/1917
War Diary	Boesinghe	24/01/1917	28/01/1917
War Diary	Roussel Fm	28/01/1917	02/02/1917
War Diary	Bleuet Fm	02/02/1917	05/02/1917
War Diary	Boesinghe	06/02/1917	09/02/1917
War Diary	Boesinghe Roussel Fm	10/02/1917	14/02/1917
War Diary	L Line Machine Gun Farm	15/02/1917	15/02/1917
War Diary	L Line	15/02/1917	28/02/1917
War Diary	L Line	01/03/1917	02/03/1917
War Diary	Bleuet Fm	03/03/1917	06/03/1917
War Diary	Boesinghe	06/03/1917	10/03/1917
War Diary	X Camp	11/03/1917	13/03/1917
War Diary	Bleuet Fm	14/03/1917	18/03/1917
War Diary	Boesinghe	19/03/1917	22/03/1917
War Diary	Bleuet Fm	22/03/1917	25/03/1917

War Diary	Boesinghe	26/03/1917	31/03/1917
War Diary	Bleuet Farm	01/04/1917	02/04/1917
War Diary	Boesinghe	03/04/1917	06/04/1917
War Diary	Bleuet Fm	07/04/1917	11/04/1917
War Diary	Bleuet Farm	11/04/1917	13/04/1917
War Diary	Boesinghe	13/04/1917	18/04/1917
War Diary	X Camp	19/04/1917	30/04/1917
War Diary	Merckeghem	01/05/1917	15/05/1917
War Diary	Herzeele	16/05/1917	18/05/1917
War Diary	L Camp	18/05/1917	18/05/1917
War Diary	Boesinghe	19/05/1917	24/05/1917
War Diary	Boesinghe Bleuet Fm	25/05/1917	28/05/1917
War Diary	Bleuet Farm	28/05/1917	30/05/1917
War Diary	Bleuet Fm	31/05/1917	31/05/1917
War Diary	Boesinghe	01/06/1917	08/06/1917
War Diary	Boesinghe Section	09/06/1917	13/06/1917
War Diary	Elverdinghe	13/06/1917	15/06/1917
War Diary	Proven	16/06/1917	26/06/1917
War Diary	Caestre	27/06/1917	27/06/1917
War Diary	Febvin-Palfart	28/06/1917	16/07/1917
War Diary	Guarbecque	17/07/1917	17/07/1917
War Diary	Caestre	18/07/1917	18/07/1917
War Diary	Eecke	19/07/1917	19/07/1917
War Diary	Proven	20/07/1917	20/07/1917
War Diary	Near St. Sixte	21/07/1917	31/07/1917
War Diary	Pilckem	30/07/1917	06/08/1917
War Diary	St. Sixte	06/08/1917	18/08/1917
War Diary	Near Boesinghe	19/08/1917	21/08/1917
War Diary	Pilckem	22/08/1917	28/08/1917
War Diary	Elverdinghe	29/08/1917	09/09/1917
War Diary	Proven	10/09/1917	12/09/1917
War Diary	Eecke	13/09/1917	13/09/1917
War Diary	Morecque	14/09/1917	14/09/1917
War Diary	Estaires	15/09/1917	15/09/1917
War Diary	Waterlands	16/09/1917	16/09/1917
War Diary	Houplines	17/09/1917	31/10/1917
War Diary	Armentiers	01/11/1917	30/11/1917
War Diary	Armentieres	01/12/1917	31/12/1917
War Diary	Witternesse Map Ref France Sheet 36 A 1/40000 N. 13 B	01/01/1918	06/01/1918
War Diary	Witternesse	07/01/1918	18/01/1918
War Diary	Guarbecque (Trance 36A. 1/40000	19/01/1918	19/01/1918
War Diary	Neuf Berquin (France 36A 1/40000 L. 14. L. 21	20/01/1918	21/01/1918
War Diary	Neuf Berquin	21/00/1918	31/01/1918
War Diary	Neuf Berquin France 36 A 40000 L14, L21	01/02/1918	11/02/1918
War Diary	Menegate Camp Sheet 36. 1/40000 B. 19. a. 3.2	12/02/1918	15/02/1918
War Diary	Menegate Camp	16/02/1918	27/02/1918

WO95/2561/3

16 Battalion Welsh Regiment

38TH DIVISION
115TH INFY BDE

16TH BN WELCH REGT
DEC 1915-FEB 1918

16th Welsh Rfs.
Vol I

12/7910

11 5/38

38 M/K/12

Dec '15
Feb '16

Army Form C. 2118

WAR DIARY
or
INTELLIGENCE SUMMARY
(Erase heading not required.)

Instructions regarding War Diaries and Intelligence Summaries are contained in F.S. Regs., Part II. and the Staff Manual respectively. Title Pages will be prepared in manuscript.

Place	Date	Hour	Summary of Events and Information	Remarks and references to Appendices
HAZELEY DOWN WINCHESTER	4/12/15	6.0 a.m.	The Battalion, 16th I.B. The Welsh Regt (Cardiff City) left Camp and marched to SOUTHAMPTON. Strength. 30 Officers. 995 other ranks. Weather Conditions - very wet.	1/2.
SOUTHAMPTON	4/12/15	2.0 p.m.	The Battalion embarked on board the S/S "La Marguerite" and sailed at 11.30 p.m. Weather Conditions very stormy and wet	1/2.
HAVRE	5/12/15	7.0 p.m.	Arrival at HAVRE at this hour. Disembarkation completed 8.15. a.m. The Battalion marched to No 5. Rest Camp.	1/2.
"	"	6.0.A.m.	The Battalion entrained at the GARE DES MARCHANDISES and departed HAVRE 9.10 p.m. Weather wet during day, fine at departure.	1/2.
ST. QUENTIN	6/12/15	10.0 p.m.	The Battalion arrived by train at AIRE SUR LYS at 6.30 p.m. detrained and marched to ST QUENTIN, where it went into billets in farms and farm buildings. Weather continually wet.	1/2.
ST QUENTIN	7/12/15	–	No Change. – weather dull	1/2.
"	8/12/15	–	" " fine	21.
"	9/12/15	–	" " Heavy rain all day.	21.
"	10/12/15	–	" " Fine	22.13.
"	11/12/15	–	" " Rain	22.13.
"	12/12/15	–	" " Showery	22.15.
"	13/12/15	–	" " Fine with frosty night	22.
"	14/12/15	"	" " "	22.
"	15/12/15	"	" " Changeable	23.
"	16/12/15	"	" " "	22.
"	17/12/15	"	" " "	25.

Army Form C. 2118

WAR DIARY
or
INTELLIGENCE SUMMARY
(Erase heading not required.)

Instructions regarding War Diaries and Intelligence Summaries are contained in F.S. Regs., Part II. and the Staff Manual respectively. Title Pages will be prepared in manuscript.

Place	Date	Hour	Summary of Events and Information	Remarks and references to Appendices
ST. QUENTIN	18/12/15		No Change. Weather fine	
do	19/12/15		" " "	
do	20/12/15		" " "	
ROBECQ	21/12/15		Marched from ST.QUENTIN at 8.30 a.m arriving at ROBECQ at 2.15. P.m	
do	22/12/15		do No Change weather rainy	
do	23/12/15		do do	
do	24/12/15		do MAJOR. F.W. SMITH sustained an accidental wound in left cheek caused by bomb explosion. He was conveyed to No 2. Clearing Hospital	
do	25/12/15		The C.O. LIEUT.COL. FRANK H.GASKELL sustained an accident by fracturing his right leg, caused by his horse falling. He was conveyed to No 2. Clearing Hospital. MAJOR.T.COCHRAN taking over command of the Battn	
do	26/12/15		No change, weather alternately wet and fine	
do	27/12/15		" " " "	
do	28/12/15		" " " "	CR
do	29/12/15		The Battalion left ROBECQ in busses and proceeded to VIEILLE CHAPELLE. where they marched to ST. VAAST and joined the 58th Brigade for instructional purposes. A.COY. (strength 5 Officers and 215 men) attached to 9th CHESHIRE.REGT. B Coy. (strength 4 Officers 216 men) attached to 9th R.W.F. C. Coy (strength 6 Officers 208 men) attached to 9th WELCH.REGT. D. Coy (strength 5 Officers and 210 men) attached to 6th WILTS.REGT. The Machine Gun party being attached to the 58th Brigade Machine Gun Party. Headquarters attached to 6th WILTS.REGT. B and C Coys remaining with their respective Battns at dusk in firing line and supports at NEUVE CHAPPELLE, A and D Coys joined their respective Battns in Brigade Reserve.	CR
ST. VAAST	30/12/15		Casualties:- C Coy 1 killed and 3 wounded from shell fire in front trench PLUMB.ST.	CR
do	31/12/15		do B " 1 killed and 3 wounded from shell fire in front trench SIGN.POST.LANE. B and C Coys were relieved at dusk by A and D Coys. B and C Coys returning to Brigade Reserve at ST.VAAST.	CR

16th Welsh Rgt.
Vol: 2

L 2
select

WAR DIARY or INTELLIGENCE SUMMARY

Army Form C. 2118

16th Battalion Welsh Regt

Place	Date	Hour	Summary of Events and Information	Remarks and references to Appendices
ST. VAAST.	1/1/16		Headquarters attached to 9th WELCH REGT.	C.R.
do	4/1/16		A. and D Coys went into the front line trenches with 6th WILTS and 9th CHESHIRES, 58th Brigade	CR
			A and D Coys came out of the front line trenches with 6th WILTS and 9th CHESHIRES this evening having had no casualties, and were attached to 8th N. STAFFS and 10th ROYAL WARWICKS, 57th Brigade respectively in reserve.	
do	5/1/16		B. and C Coys went into the front line trenches with the 10th WORCESTERS and 8th GLOUCESTERS, 57th Brigade, respectively, this evening	CR
			B and C Coys came out of the front line trenches this evening and were billetted at LES HUIT MAISONS	
do	6/1/16		The Battalion rendezvoued at ZELOBES and marched back into rest billets at ROBECQ reaching there at 2.30 pm	CR
ROBECQ	7/1/16		One man of C Coy sustained a self inflicted wound in left hand whilst cleaning his rifle	CR
do	8/1/16		No change weather rainy	CR
do	9/1/16		do " fine	CR
do	10/1/16		do " showery	CR
do	11/1/16		2Lt D.L.S.GASKELL and six men wounded by a grenade exploding prematurely, whilst at practice. One man died immediately afterwards. The others, with the exception of one man able to return to duty, were admitted to Hospital	CR
do	12/1/16		2Lt D.L.S. GASKELL died of his wounds at 1.40 a.m. The Officer was buried at ST VENANT and the man buried at the CEMETERY. ROBECQ in the portion allotted to BRITISH TROOPS. Crosses were erected and position recorded by the C of E. Chaplain.	CR
do	13/1/16		No change. Weather fine	CR
do	14/1/16		do	CR

WAR DIARY
or
INTELLIGENCE SUMMARY

(Erase heading not required.)

Army Form C. 2118

16th Battalion
Welsh Regt

Place	Date	Hour	Summary of Events and Information	Remarks and references to Appendices
ROBECQ	15/1/16		The Battalion marched from ROBECQ to the BRIGADE RESERVE at RIEZ BAILLEUL into billets	CR
RIEZ BAILLEUL	16/1/16		The Battalion marched into the front line trenches. Headquarters at EBENEZER FARM. D Coy being the first Coy to take over the left sub sector, the flank being just NORTH of MOATED GRANGE FARM. A Coy being the second Coy to take over the right sub sector, the right flank resting on SIGN POST LANE. B Coy moving in and took up the centre position. C Coy taking over posts at TILLELOY.S. LAFONE, PUMPHOUSE and BATTN. HDQTRS. D Coy moved into position at 4.30 p.m. Battalions on either flanks were 10th WARWICKS on the right and the 11th Battr. S.W.B on the left. One man of D Coy wounded.	CR
	17/1/16		2 men of C Coy wounded. 1 man of A Coy killed.	CR
	18/1/16		The Battalion was relieved. B Coy taking over the posts TILLELOY.S. LAFONE and PUMPHOUSE, this Battn taking over from the 17th R.W.F posts at ROUGE CROIX.E. with one platoon in each. Companies then marched back to billets at RIEZ.BAILLEUL by platoons at five minute intervals.	CR
	19/1/16		A draft consisting of 6. N.C.O's and 23 men arrived from ENGLAND and were posted to Coys as follows:- 2 N.C.O's and 5 men to A Coy. 2 N.C.O's and 11 men to B Coy. 1 N.C.O. and 9 men to C Coy. 1 N.C.O. and 5 men to D Coy. The Battn marched into the front line trenches and relieved the 17th R.W.F. this evening. The order of relief the same as on the 16th inst. A Coy moving in at SIGN POST LANE and B.C and D Coys by TILLELOY.S. communication trench, but any movement S or E of ROUGE CROIX and junction of RUGBY ROAD – RUE-DU-BACQUEROT before 4.30. pm being prohibited. Headquarters again at EBENEZER FARM	CR
	21/1/16		One man wounded	
	22/1/16		The Battn who relieved this evening by 17th R.W.F Companies and Machine Gunners proceeding independently to RIEZ. BAILLEUL and occupied previous billets. One man killed and one man wounded whilst leaving trenches	CR

16th Battn
Welsh Regt   Army Form C. 2118

WAR DIARY
or
INTELLIGENCE SUMMARY
(Erase heading not required.)

Instructions regarding War Diaries and Intelligence Summaries are contained in F.S. Regs., Part II. and the Staff Manual respectively. Title Pages will be prepared in manuscript.

Place	Date	Hour	Summary of Events and Information	Remarks and references to Appendices
RIEZ.BAILLEUL	23/1/16		The Battalion proceeded to CROIX MARMUSE into billets	CR
CROIX.MARMUSE	24/1/16		The Machine Gun Section proceeded to take up posts at EUSTON. SVAAST, LORETTO and GROTTO this day	CR
	25/1/16		No change weather fine	
	26/1/16		Guards for the following posts now furnished by the Battn:— A. Coy for the post EPINETTE. C. coy for the post FOSSE and RUE DU PONCH: B Coy for the post PARADIS. N: Captain H.P. HERDMAN took over the Command and pay of A Coy vice Captain J.A. RUSSELL admitted into Hospital	CR CR
	27/1/16		No change weather fine	CR
	28/1/16		do do	CR
	29/1/16		do do	CR
	30/1/16		The Battn was inspected by the Minister of Munitions the Right Hon: D. Lloyd George	CR
	31/1/16		The Battn marched into the front line trenches and relieved the 13th Battn Welsh Regt in the RIGHT SUB. SECTOR. LEFT SECTOR 115th Brigade. The disposition of the Battn being:— Battn Hdqtrs EDGWARE ROAD S.4.D.9½.7. A. Coy RIGHT S. 10. B.H.1 from MOLE STREET to LA BASSÉE ROAD inclusive. B. Coy Centre, from LA.BASSÉE ROAD to OXFORD ROAD exclusive and C Coy OXFORD ROAD to 15th STREET. S.5.D.3.9 both inclusive. D. Coy 2 platoons and H.Q's in support of RIGHT Coy at COPSE STREET and 2 platoons at Battn Hdqtrs. Reference Map 36. S.W. 3. Battalion on RIGHT flank 16th R.W.F 113th Brigade and Battn on LEFT 11th S.W.B. 115th Brigade	CR

Strength of Battn on 31st January 1916

Officers	W.O's	Sergts	Staff Sergts	Corporals	Privates	Total All ranks
26	5	46		46	910	1033

C Rowley
Capt
CAPTAIN & ADJT.
16th SER. BATTN.
THE WELSH REGIMENT

4/2/15

16th Welch Rgt.
Vol: 3

WAR DIARY or INTELLIGENCE SUMMARY

Army Form C. 2118

16th Battn Queen's Regt

(Erase heading not required.)

Place	Date	Hour	Summary of Events and Information	Remarks and references to Appendices
Reference Map 36.W.3	1/3/16		The Battalion is in the front line relieved RIGHT. SUB. SECTOR. LEFT SECTOR. R. 115th Brigade with Dispositions as follows:- Battn Hdqtrs at EDGWARE ROAD. S.14.D.94.7. A.COY. RIGHT S.10.B.4.1. from MOLE. STREET. to LABASSÉE ROAD inclusive. B. COY. CENTRE. from LABASSÉE ROAD to OXFORD ROAD exclusive less one platoon in garrison at PORT ARTHUR'S KEEP. C.COY. OXFORD ROAD to 15th STREET. S.S.D.2.9. both inclusive less one platoon at HILL 65 REDOUBT. D.COY. 2 platoons and Coy Hdqtrs in support of right Coy at COPSE STREET. and 2 platoons at Battn Hdqtrs One man wounded, died shortly afterwards	C.R
	2/3/16		3 men wounded. (bullet wounds)	C.R
	3/3/16		2 men wounded. 1 shrapnel the other bullet wound.	C.R
	4/3/16		The Battn was relieved in the front line by the 17th Battn R.W.F. and proceeded to occupy the Reserve billets vacated by them at CROIX. BARBER this evening 3 men wounded (6 shrapnel, 1 bomb, 1 bullet wound.)	C.R
CROIX. BARBER	5/3/16		Precautionary measures taken regarding disposition of the Battn in the event of an attack. Inspection of arms, ammunition, bathing of men. Clothing parties furnished for work on communication trenches. One man wounded. 2 Lieuts A.W. TAYLOR and M.G. BOSTOCK joined the Battn and take on the strength.	C.R
	6/3/16		No change. The Band proceeded to the 19th Division to play for various units.	C.R
	7/3/16		No change. One man wounded.	C.R
	8/3/16		The Battn relieved the 17th R.W.F. in the front line this evening in the RIGHT SUBSECTOR LEFT. SECTOR, 115th Brigade. Disposition as follows. D. Coy. RIGHT. S.10.B.4.1. from MOLE STREET. to LABASSÉE ROAD inclusive. B. Coy CENTRE. from LABASSÉE ROAD to OXFORD ROAD exclusive two one platoon garrison at PORT ARTHUR'S KEEP. C. COY. OXFORD ROAD	C.R

Army Form C. 2118

WAR DIARY
or
INTELLIGENCE SUMMARY
(Erase heading not required.)

Instructions regarding War Diaries and Intelligence Summaries are contained in F.S. Regs., Part II. and the Staff Manual respectively. Title Pages will be prepared in manuscript.

Place	Date	Hour	Summary of Events and Information	Remarks and references to Appendices
CROIX BARBEE	6/2/16		to 15th STREET S.5 D.2.9 took relieving also 1 platoon at HILL'S REDOUBT. A.Coy 2 platoons and Hdqtrs in support of RIGHT COY at COPSE STREET and 2 platoons at Batt Hdqtrs at EDGWARE ROAD S.4.D.9.5.7.	CR
	9/2/16		No Change	CR
	10/2/16		No Change	CR
	11/2/16		3 men wounded (1 bullet, 2 self inflicted)	CR
	12/2/16		The Battn was relieved in the trenches by the 17th Battn R.W.F. this evening and proceeded to billets at CROIX BARBEE	CR
	13/2/16		Working parties furnished for work on communication trenches inspection of Arms, ammunition, gas helmets etc. and training of men. 2 Lieuts R.E. LYNE, J.P. LLOYD and R.H. HUTCHINGS with one man joined the Battn. Captain J.A. RUSSELL and Lieut & Quartermaster A.L. ACRAMAN invalided to England 31/1/16	CR
	14/2/16		Notification of 3 men invalided to England on 31/1/16, 4/2/16 and 6/2/16 respectively, and of 2 men "died of wounds" on 1/2/16 and 5/2/16 respectively. The Band returned from the 19th Division	CR
	15/2/16		The Battn proceeded into billets at LA PANNERIE W.H.A.9.7 this day, the incoming unit to CROIX BARBEE being the 7th Battn EAST LANC'S REGT. BATTN Hdqtrs at LA PANNERIE Q.28.C.6.3.	CR
LA PANNERIE	16/2/16		No Change	CR
	17/2/16		The Battn proceeded into billets at LOGUIN W.L.D.4.4. Lieut K.H. NOEL posted to the 115th A. Field Mortar Battery and struck off strength (Authority A.G. G.H.Q. D.530/27 of 11/2/16)	CR

WAR DIARY
or
INTELLIGENCE SUMMARY
(Erase heading not required.)

Army Form C. 2118

Place	Date	Hour	Summary of Events and Information	Remarks and references to Appendices
LOCON	17/2/16		The Battn furnished garrisons consisting of 1 N.C.O. and 3 men for the following posts: MESPLAUX.E. X.15.6.2.8. MESPLAUX.N. X.8.6.9.2. LE TOURET.N.E X.17.A.6.4. RUE DE L'EPINETTE. S.13.d.4.6. CHAVETTES. S.13.6.4.7. LE TOURET. N.X.10.4.3	C R
	18/2/16		No change	C R
	19/2/16		The Battn moved into the front line trenches and relieved the 2nd Battn South Staffords Regt in the RIGHT BATTN. C.1. TIFF ROAD. A.3.C.1.6. to PIONEER ROAD. both inclusive this evening. The line taken over consisting of (A) a series of island trenches numbered 1 to 16 inclusive – No 1 to 10 RIGHT GROUP, No 11 to 16. LEFT GROUP, intercommunication between isolated breastworks only possible at night. (B) Old British line breastwork situate communication with (A) only possible at night. Ground very wet and difficult to traverse. Distances between A and B about 1200 yards. 2nd Lieut L.I. Leverock admitted to hospital (sick). The W Coy of 18th Lancashire Fusiliers attached to this Battn for instructional purposes, distributed as follows: No 1 Platoon to A Coy; No 2 to B Coy; No 3 to C Coy and No 4 to D Coy	C R
	20/2/16		2 men killed and 3 men wounded	C R
	21/2/16		one man wounded (self inflicted)	C R
	22/2/16		7 men invalided to England on various dates in January and 2 men died of wounds	C R
	23/2/16		The Battn was relieved in the front line trenches by the 17th Battn R.W.F. and proceeded into SUPPORT billets at FESTUBERT.	C R
FESTUBERT	24/2/16		Lieut H.F. DAVIES and draft of 10 men posted to the Battn and taken on the strength	C R

WAR DIARY
or
INTELLIGENCE SUMMARY
(Erase heading not required.)

Army Form C. 2118

Place	Date	Hour	Summary of Events and Information	Remarks and references to Appendices
FESTUBERT	25/2/16		Working parties furnished and inspection of arms, ammunition, clothing and gas helmets, bathing of men etc.	CR
	26/2/16		1 man of 18th Lanc's Fusiliers attached killed by shell	CR
	27/2/16		The W Cy of the 18th Lanc's Fusiliers detached from the Batt this day and the W Cy of the 14th Gloucester Regt were attached in a similar manner for instructional purposes. The Batt relieved the 11th R.W.F. in the front line trenches this evening. Right Battn C.I. 115th Brigade with 16th R.W.F. 113th Brigade on Right flank and the 11th Batt S.W.B. 115th Brigade on left flank.	CR
	28/2/16		No change. one man wounded (bullet)	CR
	29/2/16		Ditto. one man wounded (")	CR
			Strength of Battn on 29/2/16	
			Officers — W.O.'s — Sgts and Left Corpls — Corpls — Privates — Total All Ranks	
			28 — 4 — 45 — 43 — 889 — 1009	

Thomas Coleman
Major
Cmdg 16th Welsh Regt

16 Welsh Reg
vol 4

96
F

WAR DIARY
or
INTELLIGENCE SUMMARY

16th Batt~n~ Eveld. Regt. (Can. Exp. Force)

Army Form C. 2118

(Erase heading not required.)

Place	Date	Hour	Summary of Events and Information	Remarks and references to Appendices
FESTUBERT	1/3/16		No Change	LaPH
	2/3/16		The Battn. to be relieved by the 17th Batt. R.W.I. in the front line trenches this evening and the Battn. proceeded to occupy the billets at LE TOURET	LaPH
	3/3/16		No Change (Bathing of Batt~n~, inspection on arms, equipment, gasheimels and feet)	LaPH
	4/3/16		No Change	LaPH
	5/3/16		No Change	LaPH
	6/3/16		The Batt~n~ relieved the 17th R.W.I. in the front line trenches, RIGHT. BATT~N~. SUB.SECTION C.2.R.2.U. FIFE ROAD to A.3.C.7.6 PIONEER ROAD, both exclusive, the disposition of the Battn. being as follows :- A. Coy. providing garrisons for the Right Group of Islands No. 1 to 6 inclusive. - A. Coy. the Coy. being on the Right flank of the Old British Line. D. Coy. providing the garrisons for the Left Group of Islands No. 11 to 16 inclusive, the remainder of the Coy. being on the Left flank support of the O.B.L. B. Coy. manning the Left Centre support of the O.B.L. C. Coy. (2 Platoons) manning the Right Centre support of the O.B.L. 2 Sections in the Village Fort FESTUBERT	LaPH NaPH
	7/3/16		No Change	LaPH
	8/3/16		On the 2nd day of this day, the front line is held by the Battn. extended southwards as far GRENADIER. ROAD exclusive and gave up on the North. No. 16 and 14 Islands together the portion of the O.B.L. North of QUINQUE. RUE. S. 27.d.3.75. The Right and Left flanks relatively on GRENADIER. ROAD and QUINQUE. RUE, both exclusive in the O.B.L. the front line PRINCESS ISLAND to No.13 Island inclusive. D Coy taking over No's 9 and 10 Islands from A Coy and A Coy on the Right, taking over PRINCESS ISLAND from the 16th Batt~n~ R.W.I. D Coy relinquishing No's 9 and 10 Islands and part of the O.B.L. on the left to the 11 Batt~n~ S.W.B. C. Coy returning from FESTUBERT and taking over GEORGE STREET GROUSE BUTTS and 45 PLANTIN Redout trenches from 16th Batt. R.W.I. O.R. 1 killed	LaPH

Army Form C. 2118

16th Batt.
Welsh Regt.
(Cardiff City)

WAR DIARY
or
INTELLIGENCE SUMMARY
(Erase heading not required.)

Instructions regarding War Diaries and Intelligence Summaries are contained in F.S. Regs., Part II. and the Staff Manual respectively. Title Pages will be prepared in manuscript.

Place	Date	Hour	Summary of Events and Information	Remarks and references to Appendices
FESTUBERT	9/3/16		2 men killed and 2 men wounded	
	10/3/16		The Batt. was relieved by the 17th Batt. R.W.F. this evening and the Batt. proceeded to occupy the billets at FESTUBERT.	L.a.P.H.
	11/3/16		No Change (working parties, inspection of arms, equipment and gas helmets etc.)	L.a.P.H.
	12/3/16		No Change	L.a.P.H.
	13/3/16		No Change. 1 man wounded from friendly bursting of British shell (shrapnel)	L.a.P.H.
	14/3/16		The Batt. relieved the 17th Batt. R.W.F. in the front line trenches on the evening of this day, the disposition of the Batt. being :- B Coy. occupying the line from PRINCESS ISLAND to Jos Island inclusive and Right Centre O.B.L. C. Coy. LEFT ISLANDS No's 9. to 13 inclusive and left flank O.B.L. D Coy. being the Right Coy. in GEORGE STREET, GROUSE BUTTS, LE PLANTIN EAST, and VILLAGE GUARD. A. Coy CENTRE Coy. Q.A.L.	L.a.P.H.
	15/3/16		2 men wounded and one man killed	L.a.P.H.
	16/3/16		one man " " "	L.a.P.H.
LES CHOQEAUX	17/3/16		The Batt. was relieved in the front line trenches by the 17th Batt. R.W.F. on the evening of this day and proceeded to occupy billets at LESCHOQEAUX W.I.K.A. in Brigade Reserve.	L.a.P.H.
	17/3/16		Lieut Col. J.H. GASKELL resumed the Batt. on this day over Command of the Batt. and Major F.W. SMITH rejoined the Batt. and took over R.W.I. Command.	
	18/3/16		No Change (Inspection of arms, bathing, gas helmets, equipment, boots, etc.) Capt. M.L. BOYD joined the Batt. and posted to Headquarters as Gripping and Intelligence Officer	L.a.P.H.
	19/3/16		No Change	L.a.P.H.
	20/3/16		No Change	L.a.P.H.
	21/3/16		No Change	L.a.P.H.
	22/3/16		No Change	L.a.P.H.

WAR DIARY
or
INTELLIGENCE SUMMARY

(Erase heading not required.)

11th Bath. Welsh Regt (Cardiff City)

Army Form C. 2118

Instructions regarding War Diaries and Intelligence Summaries are contained in F. S. Regs., Part II. and the Staff Manual respectively. Title Pages will be prepared in manuscript.

Place	Date	Hour	Summary of Events and Information	Remarks and references to Appendices
LES CHOQEAUX	23/3/16		No Change. (Major T. COCHRAN is invalided to England and struck off the strength)	LaPH.
	24/3/16		The Batt. moved into Brigade Reserve at GORRE, relieving the 10th Batt. S.W.B.	LaPH.
GORRE	25/3/16		No Change	LaPH.
	26/3/16		No Change	LaPH.
	27/3/16		No Change	LaPH.
GIVENCHY, LEZ LA BASSEE	28/3/16		The Batt. relieved the 17th Batt. R. W. F. in the front line trenches in the RIGHT. SUB-SECTOR of the RIGHT SECTOR of the 38th Divisional Front on the evening of this day, the disposition of the Batt. being:- A. Coy. LEFT SUB-SECTOR, C Coy CENTRE SUB-SECTOR, B Coy. RIGHT SUB-SECTOR and D Coy in support in the VILLAGE LINES. The Batt. on the right being the 4th Batt. KING'S LIVERPOOL REGT. That on the left being 11th Batt. S.W.B.	LaPH. LaPH. LaPH.
	29/3/16		No Change	
	30/3/16		One man killed and four men wounded	
	31/3/16		One man killed	

Strength of the Batt. on 31/3/16

Officers	W.O's	Sergts and Staff Sergts	Corporals	Privates	Total all ranks
29	4	47	37	887	1004

WAR DIARY or INTELLIGENCE SUMMARY

Army Form C. 2118

6th Battn.

Place	Date	Hour	Summary of Events and Information	Remarks and references to Appendices
GIVENCHY LEZ LA BASSEE	1/4/16		The Battn. who relieved by the 17th Battn. R.W.F. on the evening of this day and the Battn moved into Support billets at GIVENCHY LEZ LA BASSEE.	
	2/4/16		2 men killed. Clothing parties furnished on front line trenches	
	3/4/16		" "	
	4/4/16		" " 2 men killed and 3 men wounded	
	5/4/16		The Battn. relieved the 17th Battn. R.W.F. in front line trenches on the evening of this day, the disposition of the front line trenches being B Coy. Right Sector, C Coy. Centre Sector, D Coy. Left Sector. A Coy. in Support Village. Right flank being the 11th Battn. L.W.R. on the left the Battn on the left flank being the 11th Battn. L.W.R. on the right, the 9th Queen's Own Surreys. 2 men killed	
	6/4/16		2 men wounded. Lieut. M. G. Pettigrew R.A.M.C. slightly wounded, but remained on duty	
	7/4/16		No Change	
	8/4/16		A raid was attempted against a hostile Machine Gun Emplacement at A.6.C.53.6.6. The wire cutting party completed its task and succeeding in placing a "torpedo" in position. Unfortunately at the last moment the raiding party who discovered machine gun and rifle fire being turned upon them making it necessary to retire. 2 Lieut. O.M. WILLIAMS missing and wounded, believed dead. 1 man wounded missing believed dead. 3 men wounded	

WAR DIARY or INTELLIGENCE SUMMARY

Army Form C. 2118

2
6th Battn.
Tudor. Regt
(East Kent GH)

Place	Date	Hour	Summary of Events and Information	Remarks and references to Appendices
GIVENCHY LEZ LA BASSEE	9/4/16		The Battn. was relieved by the 17th Battn. R.W.F. on the evening of this day and the Battn. proceeded into billets at LES CHOQUAUX in Brigade Reserve	X.
LES CHOQUAUX	10/4/16		Working parties furnished. Inspection of arms, clothing equipment etc	X.
	11/4/16		No change	X.
	12/4/16		" one man wounded	X.
	13/4/16		"	X.
NEUF BERQUIN ESTAIRES	14/4/16		The Battn. moved into billets at NEUF BERQUIN ESTAIRES this day and garrisoned posts at WANGERIE with 1 Officer and 2 platoons, ESQUIN with 1 Officer and 1 platoon, MASSELOT with 1 platoon, ROAD BEND with 1 Officer and 1 platoon, MASSELOT HOUSE with 1 Section and O.R.A HOUSE with 1 Section	X.
	15/4/16		The Battn. moved into Right Support at LAVENTIE this day. one man wounded	X.
LAVENTIE	16/4/16		No change	X.
	17/4/16		"	X.
	18/4/16		"	X.
	19/4/16		The Battn. relieved the 17th Battn. R.W.F. in the front line trenches in the Right Sub-Sector Right Centre. C Coy left battn. A Coy on the Right. D Coy	X.
	20/4/16		2 men wounded, 1 man killed	X
	21/4/16		1 man wounded	X.

(3)

Army Form C. 2118

16th Battn. Regt.
Welsh Regt.
(Cardiff City)

WAR DIARY
or
INTELLIGENCE SUMMARY
(Erase heading not required.)

Place	Date	Hour	Summary of Events and Information	Remarks and references to Appendices
LAVENTIE	22/4/16		2 men wounded	9%
	23/4/16		2 men wounded	
			The Battn. moved into billets at LAVENTIE this evening and the following Coys. were garrisoned	
			C Coy. MASSELOT, WANGERIE ROAD BEND, MASSELOT HOUSE and C.R.A. HOUSE. D Coy. took up	
			at ESQUIN POST. A Coy in "Close Support" at the GENDARMERIE. B Coy in billets	1/2
			at SANG TENATIE LAVENTIE.	
	24/4/16		1 man killed	1/2
	25/4/16		No Change	2/2
	26/4/16		No Change	2/2
	27/4/16		The Battn. relieved the 17th Battn. R.W.F. this evening in the front line trenches of	
			the Right Sub Section. The disposition of the Battn. being the same as on the 19th inst	9/2
			one man wounded	
	28/4/16		12 men wounded. 1 remained on duty. 1 died shortly afterwards, one man killed	2/2
	29/4/16		1 man wounded, 1 man killed	2/2
	30/4/16		2 men wounded	2/2
			Strength of the Battn. on 30/4/16	
			Officers. W.O's. Sergts. Staff Sgts. Corpls. Privates. Total	
			33 5 46 46 893 1024	1/2

1875 Wt. W593/826 1,000,000 4/15 J.B.C. & A. A.D.S.S./Forms/C. 2118.

XXXVIII Army Form C. 2118
Sheet No. 1.   10th Battalion
             Welsh Regt.
             (Cardiff City)   Vol 6

WAR DIARY or INTELLIGENCE SUMMARY
(Erase heading not required.)

Instructions regarding War Diaries and Intelligence Summaries are contained in F. S. Regs., Part II. and the Staff Manual respectively. Title Pages will be prepared in manuscript.

Place	Date	Hour	Summary of Events and Information	Remarks and references to Appendices
La Gorgue	1/5/16	8.a.m.	Battalion Bathing, commencing with B. Coy. followed by C.D & A & Headquarters	TWJ
		10/a.m.	Inoculation of Battn. commencing with B. Coy.	TWJ
	2/5/16		Working parties found by A, B & D. Coys.	TWJ
		11.30 a.m.	Completion of bathing	TWJ
	3/5/16	6.a.m.	Inspection of Transport & Battn. Billets by C. O. C.	TWJ
		10/a.m.	Working party found by A. Coy.	
	4/5/16	10/a.m.	Inoculation of N.C.O's & men who have not been already inoculated	TWJ
			Battn. Bombers Parade.	
			Draft from England 19 men	
		11.30 a.m.	Inspection of L Coy by Commanding Officer	
			Reconnaissance of approaches to front line by all Officers.	
		4.30 p.m.	Lecture by Regt. Sgt. Major to all N.C.O's	
			Pte Tallis 23832 wounded whilst going a course of Machine-Gun Duty	TWJ
	5/5/16	9/0 a.m.	Inspection of Saws, periscopes special articles, by Commanding Officer	TWJ
			Lecture to Boys by men who underwent a course in Gas instruction at AIRE	
	6/5/16		Accident by premature bursting of Rifle Grenade: 2nd Lt Shives & 8 men injured	TWJ
			Court of Enquiry into Grenade Accident on 5/5/16. President. Capt Hardman, Members. Fitzpatrick and Williams.	
	7/5/16		Inspection of Boys made Company Commanders	
			Church Parade. Church of England in Divisional Theatre. Roman Catholic Church of St. Peters	TWJ
	8/5/16	8/4.5 a.m.	Nonconformists. The Square.	
			Battn. head for route march Adj: in command. Route, LA GORGUE, LESTREM, FOSSE, ZELOBES,	TWJ
			CROIX MARMEUSE, L. EPPINET, Road junction R.8.b.3.4. LESTREM STATION, LA GORGUE.	
		9.30 a.m.	All Officers not on march accompanied Col: F. H. Gaskell on a tactical exercise	
			without troops.	
			Coy Commanders visited Billets at RIEZ BAILLEUL previous to Battn. moving in	
Riez Bailleul	9/5/16	3.p.m.	Battalion moved to Rue 3 Bailleul and took over following posts :—	TWJ

Sheet No 2.

WAR DIARY 16th Battalion
or
INTELLIGENCE SUMMARY Welsh Regt.
(Erase heading not required.) (Cardiff City)

Army Form C. 2118

Instructions regarding War Diaries and Intelligence Summaries are contained in F.S. Regs., Part II. and the Staff Manual respectively. Title Pages will be prepared in manuscript.

Place	Date	Hour	Summary of Events and Information	Remarks and references to Appendices
Rue Bacheul (contd)	9/5/16		A Coy. LUDIANA; B Coy 2 Pls. LUDIANA; 1 Pln. ROUGE CROIX EAST; 1Pln. ROUGE CROIX WEST; C. Coy. RIEZ BAILLEUL; D. Coy. 1 Pln. Reserve Line of 3 Platoons, RIEZ BAILLEUL; one N.C.O & men of each of the following posts. ETON, HARROW, CHELTENHAM. Working parties found by A. & C. Coys. President Capt. Howell with Lt. Carne Jones. Court of Enquiry into loss of Officers Kit.	2nd
		2/0 p.m.	" " under residence of Capt Herdman. (wounded)	2nd
	10/5/16		Relief of 10 Battn. Welsh Regt. completed. RIGHT SUPPORT BATTN. MOATED GRANGE SECTOR	2nd
		8/0 a.m.	A. Coy. Bombers paraded at 9/30 A.M.	
	11/5/16		B Battn. commenced bathing. C. Coy. first Working parties found by 10. C. & A. Coys.	2nd
	12/5/16	9/30 a.m.	Headquarters & transport bathing "C" Coy Bombers paraded Coy Commanders & Coy Sgt Majors visited Line previous to taking over.	2nd
Moated Grange Sector	13/5/16	5/0 p.m.	Working parties found by D.C. & A. Coys. All Officers attending lecture of Commanding Officer. Sup. Sector (MOATED GRANGE SECTOR) The Battn. relieved the 11th R.W.F. in the 10. Coy. Working parties for baths found as follows:- C. Coy Right Flank. D. Centre. A. Left Flank. B. LUDIHANA & LAFONE Battalion Situated as follows:- STREET HQRS at EBENEZER FARM.	2nd
	14/5/16		BATTN. HQRS at EBENEZER FARM. Working parties found by B &10 Coys "Stand - to" 2/15 A.M. Lt. FOSTER No. C. Cy. and two men slightly wounded.	2nd
	15/5/16	2/15 a.m.	Working parties B &10 Coys. "Stand -to"	2nd
	16/5/16	2/15 a.m.	"Stand -to" Lt. Col. F.H. Gaskell wounded whilst reading Sentries at Ducks Bill CRATER. Lt. Hutchings wounded whilst helping to convey Lt. Col. Gaskell from CRATER. Colvin ON 2 men wounded. B & 10 Coys furnished Working parties Cessation of Sleeping in Dug-outs.	2nd

Sheet No 5

WAR DIARY or INTELLIGENCE SUMMARY
(Erase heading not required.)

16th Battalion
Welsh Regt
(Cardiff City)

Army Form C. 2118

Place	Date	Hour	Summary of Events and Information	Remarks and references to Appendices
Moated Grange SECTOR	17/5/16		Lt. Col. F.H. Gaskell died of wounds at No.2 C.C.S. Merville. Successors furnished for A.O.D. workshops trade test. Ptes. Cooks, Hughes, Parsons. 1 Officer sent for Lewisgun Instruction at ABERVILLE. 2nd Lt. A.W. Taylor. Working parties found.	2nd
R.15z BAILLEUL	18/5/16 2.0 P.M.		The Battn relieved by the 17th R.W.F. "H" Coy remained at LUDIMANA & LAFONE Streets. B, C & D Coys returned to billets at R.15z BAILLEUL. C. Coy garrisoned BOUGE CROIX EAST & WEST. Post. ETON. HARROW & CHELTENHAM. Funeral of Lt. Col. Gaskell at MERVILLE. MAJOR F.W. SMITH, Capt & Adjt. J.B. Harris R.S.M., Hamis, (Bandmaster) 1 Officer No. Coy, Sgt Majors, Pte Mullane (of Gaskells servant) to Hamor, Pte Coggins (Col's Groom) all of whom attended the funeral. A.O.D. workshops trade test. L/Sgt J. Jones left Johnson. Batts baths. Court Martial trial of 18169 Sgt. C. Harris. Found guilty & reduced to ranks.	2nd
	19/5/16		Working parties. Parade of C. Coy Bombers. Bathing.	2nd
	20/5/16		A Draft of 144 men received from 38th Divisional C.Schl. Medical Inspection of these men by M.O. Working Parties.	3rd
	21/5/16		Parade of Church Service. Church of England 10.50 a.m. Holy Communion 11.0. R.M. nonconformist Service 11/30 a.m. Roman Catholic Service at 10/30 a.m. The Battalion relieved the 14th Battn R.W.F. in the Moated Grange Sector at 9/30 P.M. B. Coy left Flank. C. Coy right Flank. D. Coy Centre. A. Coy in R.15z LUDIMANA & LAFONE Street. Capt N.L. Angus took over duties of Second-in-command.	2nd
MOATED GRANGE SECTOR	22/5/16		Working Parties. Enemy active with Artillery & Grenades.	2nd

Sheet No. 1.

WAR DIARY
or
INTELLIGENCE SUMMARY.
(Erase heading not required.)

Army Form C. 2118.

XXXVIII
10th Bain
Welch Regt. (Cardiff City Bn.)
Vol 7

Instructions regarding War Diaries and Intelligence Summaries are contained in F. S. Regs., Part II. and the Staff Manual respectively. Title pages will be prepared in manuscript.

Place	Date	Hour	Summary of Events and Information	Remarks and references to Appendices
LA GORGUE	1916			
	31st May	8.6 am	"A" & "B" Coys continued Coy training at L.32 central. Three machine guns accompany "A" Coy. Coy inspection every evening of water bottles & iron rations to ensure that loads are filled & non rations are added. Steel helmets exchanged for those of a more shining surface.	1st Welsh Ack. M. Smith
			2nd Lucas taken on strength of Battalion, posted to "C" Coy.	M. Smith
	2nd Jun		Battn took part in Brigade route march commencing 11/15 a.m. Some of the men in billets extended from 1/0 to 9/10 p.m. 140. B.O. 1599 May 30th 1916.	M. Smith
	3rd "		Steel helmets to be regarded as personal equipment.	M. Smith
			Coy Officer's inspection of billets. Sick parade at 7/30 a.m.	
	4th "		Church Services for C.E.'s Nonconformists & Catholics.	M. Smith
			"A" Coy detailed 1 N.C.O. & 3 men to report as working party to C.R.E. at Bandstand.	
			Temp. Capt L-A Harris promoted Adjutant of the Battn. vice Temp. Capt C. Corley evacuated Sick.	
			"B" Coy provided 1 Officer, 100 O.R. working party at No. 3 Timber Yard L.34 & S.9 at 8/6 a.m.	
LAVENTIE	5th "		Battn relieved the 15th R.W.F. at LA VENTIE & took over allotted posts.	M. Smith
	6th "		2/4th Oxfords & Bucks Battn attached for instruction. Three men returned to duty from C.R.S.	B.O. 11 M. Smith
			Battn relieved 13th Battn. held Regt in right Reserve Billets at LA VENTIE	
			Received draft of 5th M.G.O's and men for duty in event of telephonic communication being suspended or cut. Formation of party of Emergency Runners.	M. Smith
	7th "		Working radio found by A.B & D Coys Machine Gunners & Snipers. Mackintosh capes handed in.	M. Smith
	8th "		Mackintosh capes handed in.	M. Smith
	9th "		Notification of Return of Capt Henig to England on 28/5/16. Working party found by "B" Coy.	M. Smith
			"B" Coy 2/4th Bucks Regt attached for instruction; also Machine Gun Section Battn relieved 17th R.W.F. Battn in right subsection of the line. This relief was subsequently cancelled	M. Smith
LA GORGUE	10th "		Relief 17th R.W.F. being cancelled Battn. moved into billets at LA GORGUE. In billets and supports Posts LA VENTIE by 2/4th of Leicesters having been relieved.	M. Smith
	11th "		Weight of Officers baggage to be reduced to a minimum of 35 lbs./m Establishment. Band to act as Stretcher Bearers from this date.	M. Smith

Sheet No 2.

WAR DIARY
or
INTELLIGENCE SUMMARY.
(Erase heading not required.)

Army Form C. 2118.

Instructions regarding War Diaries and Intelligence Summaries are contained in F. S. Regs., Part II. and the Staff Manual respectively. Title pages will be prepared in manuscript.

Place	Date	Hour	Summary of Events and Information	Remarks and references to Appendices
ROBECQ	1916. 11th June		Battn. moved into billets at ROBECQ this day.	Smith Field
	12th "		Inspection of Arms, equipments & Billets by Coy Commanders.	S.M.Smith
	13th "	7/0 am 4/40 pm	Battn. paraded for Physical drill. Inspection of Arms Equipment & Billets, extended order drill, bayonet fighting	S.M.Smith
		11/0 am	Memorial service to late Lord Kitchener.	S.M.Smith
AUCHEL	14th "		Battn. moved into billets at AUCHEL.	S.M.Smith
MONCHY BRETON	15th "		Seventeen men rejoined Battn. from various units to remain with Battn. until further orders.	S.M.Smith
	16th "		Battn. moved into billets at MONCHY BRETON	S.M.Smith
		9/0 am	Battn. paraded at 9/0 am & marched to Divl. Training Ground to practice extended order drill and artillery formation.	S.M.Smith
			G.O.C. 115th Bde held Conference with O.C. Battns. 115th Bde at CHELERS.	S.M.Smith
			Short precautions enforced against fires in billets.	S.M.Smith
	17th "	6/0 6/40 am	Battn. paraded for Physical drill	S.M.Smith
		9/0 am 4/30 pm	Battn. marched to training ground for training as per Bde programme - Coy training, attacks etc. S.M.Smith
			Signallers - Visual training in the field.	
	18th "		Received draft of six men from Base	S.M.Smith
			Lieut. T.K. Bonsall joined Battn. Posted to "C" Coy.	S.M.Smith
		9/45-11/6 am	Church parades for C. of E. Nonformists & R.C.s.	S.M.Smith
			G.O.C. 115th Bde attended conference of all Officers of Battn. at 2.30 P.M. at Battn. HQrs Mess.	S.M.Smith
			Platoon Officers delivered lecture to their platoons following G.O.C. Conference.	S.M.Smith
	19th "		Two men joined Battn. Three others rejoined Battn. from R.E. R.S.	S.M.Smith
			One N.C.O. & one man attended a course for two days Aeroplane Signalling at 13th Squadron R.F.C.	
	20th "	6/0 am	Battn. paraded for physical drill.	S.M.Smith
		9/0 am	Battn. paraded for practice at trainingshed as per programme. All available men attended	S.M.Smith
		8/15 am	training	
		9/0 1/0	Battalion paraded for Physical drill	

WAR DIARY or INTELLIGENCE SUMMARY.

Army Form C. 2118.

Place	Date	Hour	Summary of Events and Information	Remarks and references to Appendices
MONCHY BRETON	1916 June 20th	9/30 am — 6.4/30 pm	Battn. marched to Bde Training Area "C" for training as per programme - Coy training Bayonet fighting etc. One man detailed for guard at Batn. Stores, which moved in event of sudden forward move he left behind at Hythe drill.	
	21st	6/0 - 7/0 9/30 am - 6.4/30 pm	Battn. paraded for Physical drill. Battn. paraded & marched to Manoeuvre Area for training as per programme. Signallers - Visual training in the field. Officers Conference at 8 P.M. at H. Qrs. Mess. Two men permanently attached to 88th Divn. Infy. Base depot ETAPLES (D.R.O No 184)	
	22nd	6/0 - 7/0 am 9/30 - 4.30 pm	Battn. paraded for Physical drill. Battn. paraded & marched to 115th Bde Area 3 for training as per programme - Battn. attack practice. Consolidation of ground won etc. Signallers - visual training in the field. One man attd. from Divisional Signalling / B Sqdn. R.F.C. Four men rejoined Battn. from various units.	
	23rd	9/30 to 4/0 p.m.	Battn. paraded for training at 115th Bde Area 2 - Battn. attack practice taking & immediating of enemy lines. Signallers trained in Visual Signalling.	
	24th	9/0 am 6.4/30 pm	Battn. paraded & marched to Bde training Area No.1. for training as per Bde Scheme Lt. J. N. Williams + two men returned from 10nd Bayonet fighting Gymnastic Class. Nine men rejoined Battn. from 123rd Coy Field R.E.	
	25th	9/0 - 4/30 pm	Battn. paraded & marched to 10nd training as per Divn. Scheme - Signallers paraded with the Battn.	
		8/0 - 9/0 pm	Divn. Orders of two rations. Officers' Conference at H.Q. Mess	
	26th	4/15 pm	Independent parade by Coys. for inspection of arms, equipment & kits by Coy Commanders Battn. paraded and marched via TERNAS, BUNEVILLE, PT. HOUVIN NUNCQ, LIGNY-SUR-CANCHE, VACQUERIE-LE-BOURQ to FORTEL during night of 26/27th June 1916.	

Sheet 10 A

Army Form C. 2118.

WAR DIARY
or
INTELLIGENCE SUMMARY.
(Erase heading not required.)

Place	Date	Hour	Summary of Events and Information	Remarks and references to Appendices
	1916			
FORTEL	27th June		Battalion arrived FORTEL. Paraded at 4/4.5 p.m. and marched during night 27/28th to AUTHEUX via BARLY & OUTREBOIS.	2/7 O'ntt Ltd 2/7 D'nitt
AUTHEUX	28th "		Battn Billeted at AUTHEUX Inspection of Billets, arms & equipment.	2/7 D'nitt
"	29th "		Coy inspections of Billets, Arms & Equipment. Capt J.R. Hornell rejoined Battn from First Army School of Instruction and took over command of "D" Coy at COYOUTEN COURT. Battn held to entrain at 2.0 COYOUTEN COURT.	2/7 D'nitt 2/7 D'nitt
COYOUTEN COURT	30th		No 23437 Pte M. Regan 1 No 2311 Pte L.G. Little No 10071 Pte L.W. Hargrow were this day transferred to 3/7 W. Infy Depôt under Army Council Instruction 1186 13/6/16, being under age.	2/7 D'nitt
			Strength of the Battn 30/6/16	
			Officers N.C.Os Serjts & Staff Serjts Corpls Privates Total all ranks	
			44 + 46 + 44 + 980 = 1118	

115th Inf.Bde.
38th Div.

WAR DIARY

16th BATTN. THE WELCH REGIMENT.

J U L Y

1 9 1 6

Sheet 1.

WAR DIARY 16/Welch Regt.
or (Cardiff City Battn)
INTELLIGENCE SUMMARY.
(Erase heading not required.)

Army Form C. 2118.

Place	Date	Hour	Summary of Events and Information	Remarks and references to Appendices
TOUTENCOURT	1916 July 1st		Battn. in Futinent	
	2nd		Bn paraded for inspection of arms & equipment.	
ACHEUX	"		Bn moved to ACHEUX, arriving at 12 M.N. Under Canvas	
	3rd.		Inspection of arms, equipment & bivouac tents	
BUIRE S/L'ANCRE			Bn moved to BUIRE S/L'ANCRE. Under Canvas	
	4th		Inspection of Arms, equipment, Gas Helmet, goggles & lines.	
CARNOY.	5th		Brigade moved at 1.30 p.m. via MEAULTE, BECORDEL BECOURT to CARNOY. Bivouacs from BECORDEL-BECOURT. Brigade moved by Battns at half hour intervals	
	6th		Inspection of arms & equipment.	
	6th		Party of 8 Officers & in three groups sent out as Reconnaissance Patrols to reconnoitre approaches to new British position at QUEEN'S NULLAH. Partly heavily shelled; 2 officers killed, two wounded.	
	6th		Letter read from Genl. Sir Ivor Philipps to units of 38th Division. In evening Battn. proceeded via CARNOY, TRIANGLE, LOOP, LOOP TRENCH, MONTAUBAN ALLEY, r. CATERPILLAR TRENCH to Valley N. of CATERPILLAR WOOD. Between there & MAMETZ WOOD there was a slope which hid them from enemy's view;	
	7th	8.30 am.	Bn. under orders drew up on their own side of slope facing MAMETZ WOOD in	

Army Form C. 2118.

WAR DIARY
or
INTELLIGENCE SUMMARY.
(Erase heading not required.)

Instructions regarding War Diaries and Intelligence Summaries are contained in F. S. Regs., Part II. and the Staff Manual respectively. Title pages will be prepared in manuscript.

Place	Date	Hour	Summary of Events and Information	Remarks and references to Appendices
	7th		lines of platoons with a 2 platoon frontage. 11/S.W.B. in support. 15/S.W.B. in reserve. Our Artillery ceased firing at wood at 8.30 a.m., & first lines of Bn. proceeded over the crest of the slope, but came instantly under heavy Machine gun fire from MARTINPUICH, & enfilade fire from FLATIRON COPSE & SABOT COPSE & the German Second System, which ran between MARTINPUICH & BAZENTIN LE PETIT WOOD. Bn. suffered heavily, & had to withdraw to their own side of crest. Bn. made two more attacks, but position was much too exposed for any hope of success, & orders were received to cease operations. 11/S.W.B. attempted to approach the wood through a gulley running between CATERPILLAR WOOD & slope mentioned above, but Machine gun fire drove them back. Our losses :- 6 offrs. killed, 6 wounded, 268 O.R.'s killed, missing & wounded. Weather very wet, this adding greatly to exhaustion of troops. Bn. received orders to return to their Bivouac. Moved off 10.30 pm. Arrived 4. a.m. 8th.	
	8th		Roll Call at Noon. Note of appreciation on behaviour of troops from Brig. Genl. Evans communicated to Batt. Verbal	
	10th		Bn. "stood to" at 3.0 a.m. as Reserve to 113 & 114 Inf. Bdes., who attacked MARTINPUICH WOOD from South, with success but heavy casualties. About 9 p.m. Bn. received orders to reinforce 113 & 114 Bdes. in MARTINPUICH WOOD. Reaches wood	

WAR DIARY
or
INTELLIGENCE SUMMARY.
(Erase heading not required.)

Army Form C. 2118.

Place	Date	Hour	Summary of Events and Information	Remarks and references to Appendices
	10th 11th	10	about 11 p.m., reported to Brig. Genl. Marden, under whose orders they operate until arrival of Brig. Genl. Evans the following morning, under Genl. Evans instructions Bn. took up position along Railway running through western side of Wood, with their right flank about 300 yards from N. end of Wood. On the right of Bn. were 17/R.W.F., on left the 15th & 13th R.W.F., on Eastern side of Central drive through the wood were 10th & 11th S.W.B. The line was subsequently altered, so that Bn. held a position parallel with Northern edge of wood at about 300 yards distance from N. of wood: 17/R.W.F. on their right running as far as a central drive: 15/Welch R. on their left, & 16/R.W.F. relieved 13/R.W.F. The line swung itself in. Line received orders to advance to Northern, North eastern & North western edges of Wood, attack to start 3 P.M. but 20 mins before 3 P.M. our Artillery set up terrific barrage which caused few casualties to Officers & O.R.S. & Bn. rather shaken 10th Welch moved forwards later in the afternoon to the North Western line of the wood, but owing to weakness in numbers of the 17/R.W.F. our Batt. had orders to hold the line, & proceeded to inform their position. 6 P.M. Enemy commenced to bombard our position with 5.9"s & left their up ceaselessly, after		

Army Form C. 2118.

4.

WAR DIARY
or
INTELLIGENCE SUMMARY.
(Erase heading not required.)

Instructions regarding War Diaries and Intelligence Summaries are contained in F.S. Regs., Part II. and the Staff Manual respectively. Title pages will be prepared in manuscript.

Place	Date	Hour	Summary of Events and Information	Remarks and references to Appendices
	12th		dark 10/Welsh returned to original line, having been driven back by Minenwerfer, thereafter in addition to H.g's enemy bombarded our front with 700 Yellow Minenwerfer. This lasted incessantly until Batt. was relieved at about 6am by C.O. of the Northumberland Fusiliers, 31/Div. Batt. returned to bivouac under heavy shellfire. Casualties:- 10 Off. killed 2 Officers wounded. 3 Officers suffering from shell shock 67 O.R.s killed & wounded.	
WARLOY.	13th	4.30 AM 4.30 AM	Brigade moved off to WARLOY, via MEAULTE, BUIRE s/ANCRE, RIBEMONT. Arrived WARLOY 12 Noon. Batt. in billets.	
COUIN.		6 P.M.	Batt. transported by Motor lorries to COUIN. Arrived 11.30 P.M. Bivouac.	
	14th	11.45 AM 11.45 AM	Batt. addressed by Lieut. General HUNTER-WESTON, Comndg 8th Army Corps.	
HEBUTERNE Sectn		3. P.M.	Batt. moved via COURCELLES & COLINCAMPS to relieve 8/Worcester Regt (48/Div) in night sub-sector of line. (HEBUTERNE SECTION.)	
	15th		Quiet. Clearing of approaches to front line commenced, also building & wiring of strong points in front line, (which had been destroyed by recent heavy bombardment.	
	16th		Quiet. Above work continued.	
	17th		" " . Enemy machine guns & trench Mortars active at times.	

WAR DIARY
or
INTELLIGENCE SUMMARY.
(Erase heading not required.)

Army Form C. 2118.

Place	Date	Hour	Summary of Events and Information	Remarks and references to Appendices
	18th	2.40 A.M.	Party of 2 Offr. & 44 O.R's made a raid on Enemy Lines. Encountered strong working Party, who retired to their lines after some time, whereupon our Party bombed them with success, & returned to own lines. Casualties 2 O.R. wounded 4 O.R's missing. Heavy rain; trenches in very bad state. Work of repairing very difficult. Parties	
COURCELLES.	19th	4.P.M.	Bn. relieved by 17/R.W.F. Bn. returned to COURCELLES to Billets.	
	20th	Mng.	Inspection of Arms, Equipment, Billets &c. Working Party found for wiring front line.	
			Batt. baths 2 at COUIN.	
		Aft.	Working Parties sent to work under orders of 17/R.W.F.	
		Night	Wiring Parties " " " "	
	21st		Coy. Pay. Inspection Arms Equipment Billets &c.	
			Working & Wiring Parties as on 20th.	
HÉBUTERNE Sect.	22nd	4.30pm	Batt. relieves 17/R.W.F. in line. Enemy Artillery active.	
			Working parties engage clearing front line.	
	23rd		Enemy Art'y active, also French Tota. Usual working parties, also working parties from 17/R.W.F. & 113/Brigade.	
	24th		Quiet during day. Hostile Artillery, French Tota's active during night. Usual working.	

Army Form C. 2118.

WAR DIARY
or
INTELLIGENCE SUMMARY.
(Erase heading not required.)

Place	Date	Hour	Summary of Events and Information	Remarks and references to Appendices
	24th		Wiring parties from our Batt. & 17/R.W.F.	
	25th		Usual working & wiring parties	
		11 P.M.	Patrol went out to examine German wire & state of line. Found a strong wiring party. Wire evidently strongly held.	
	26th	M'n'g	Early (5.0 am) heavy German bombardment on right of our sector. Usual working parties.	
COURCELLES.	27th	4.30 P.M.	Bn. relieved by 17/R.W.F. & returned to Billets at COURCELLES. Inspection of arms & equipment. Sanitary party found working & wiring Bn. Hutments	
			Line	
VAUCHELLES.	28th	5 p.m.	Bn relieved by 6/Shropshire Light Infantry	
		12 noon	Bn. moved to VAUCHELLES, via BERTRANCOURT, BUS-LES-ARTOIS & LOUVENCOURT. Arrived 2 P.M. In Huts.	
	29th		Inspection of Huts, arms, equipment &c.	
	30th	7 am	Batt. moved to bivouac between BEAUVAL & CANDAS. Arrived 1.0 P.M.	
CANDAS		9.30 P.M.	" proceeded to CANDAS STATION. Heat intense.	
ST OMER	31st	1.50 AM	" left by train for ST OMER. Detrained at ST OMER, 9.30 A.M., & marched via	
MILLAM.			WATTEN to MILLAM. & Billets. Heat intense.	

10/Welch Regt.

Army Form C. 2118.

WAR DIARY
or
INTELLIGENCE SUMMARY.
(Erase heading not required.)

August 1916.   Vol 9

Place	Date	Hour	Summary of Events and Information	Remarks and references to Appendices
MILLAM	1916 Aug. 1		Coy Inspections.	
	2		Bathing in Canal; washing clothing.	
	3	4.30am	Brigade moved via Bergues, Bath to MERCKEGHEM. Brigade 10th KSLB & 8th LEEZEELE, 17th R.F.	
MERCKEGHEM	4		Batt. billets in MERCKEGHEM 6 am.	
			Commencement of Training, including specials as Snipers, L.M.Gunners, bombers.	
	5		Signalled Training continued.	
	6		do.	
	7		Training. Route March.	
	8		Bathing at ZEGGER's CAPPEL. Training.	
	9	morn.	Training.	
	10	aft.	Platoon Transport Lewis Gun Competitions judged by Major Dewey (18th Training (R) Rifles)	
	11		Training. Cleaning up for G.O.C's Inspection.	
	12		Inspection by G.O.C 115th Inf. Bde.	9 & 8
	13		Church Parades.	1 sheet

16 Welch Regt.   Sheet 2.
August 1916.

Army Form C. 2118.

WAR DIARY
INTELLIGENCE SUMMARY.
(Erase heading not required.)

Place	Date 1916	Hour	Summary of Events and Information	Remarks and references to Appendices
MERKEGHEM	August 14		Training	
	15		" Bn. to D.	
	16		" Bombing & Bayonet fighting in afternoon any training area	
	17		" do.	
	18		" do.	
	19	7am	1st Batt. 400 of Bn. including H.Qrs. moved to BOLLEZEELE, entraining there	
POPERINGHE			for POPERINGHE. Arrived there at 12.15pm. Remainder of Bn. arrived 2.20pm. Transport brigaded at BOLLEZEELE & proceeded by Road	
		9.30pm	Bn. left POPERINGHE 9.30pm for Asylum Station, YPRES. That there by guides	MAP. ST JULIEN 28NW
YPRES			from the 1st King's Own (Lancaster) Regt. Proceeded to line & relieved the 1st King's Own	HQrs C2026.
	19/20		Regt. in line	
	20		Line quiet	
	21		" " Gas Alert	
	22		" " a.o. Gas Alarm	
	23		Relieved by 17/R.W.F. 2 Companies quartered on Canal Bank. HQrs	C2 Central.
			& 2 Companies at L8 Machine Gun Farm.	

Welch Regt.   Sheet 3.

Army Form C. 2118.

WAR DIARY
INTELLIGENCE SUMMARY
(Erase heading not required.)

August 1916.

Instructions regarding War Diaries and Intelligence Summaries are contained in F. S. Regs., Part II. and the Staff Manual respectively. Title pages will be prepared in manuscript.

Place	Date 1916 August	Hour	Summary of Events and Information	Remarks and references to Appendices
YPRES	24		Working Parties on Canal Bank & on Vlamy Points.	
	25.		ditto. "A" Coy. from Machine Gun in Line.	
	26		Parties proceeded to HQrs 17/R.W.F. as reserve to Bn in Line. Working Parties on Canal Bank and on Vlamy Points.	
	27 Night		Relieved 17/R.W.F. in the line. One Coy 17/R.W.F. left in the line at Bn. H.Qrs.	
	28		Quiet. Working Parties on repairing & cleaning trenches.	
	29		Very wet. Heavy support trenches flooded, all men engaged on pumping & clearing	
	30		" to "	
	31. Night		Relieved by 17/R.W.F. B Coy left at Bn H.Qrs. 17/R.W.F. A Coy to H.Qrs. 2 to Machine Gun Farm. C & D Coys to Canal Bank.	

A166.   16/Welch Regt.

To 13/Inf.Bde.

   Herewith copy of War
Diary for the month of
September 1916.

                      H.P.Jones 2Lt.
                      a/adjt.
                      for O/C 16/Welch Regt
30.9.16

WAR DIARY *or* **INTELLIGENCE SUMMARY.**

(Erase heading not required.)

Army Form C. 2118.

September 1916.

VOL 10

Place	Date 1916	Hour	Summary of Events and Information	Remarks and references to Appendices
Bn. H.Q. Machine Gun Fm.	Sept. 1		Working Parties on Canal Bank & Tarry Points.	Map BELGIUM. 28.N.W. 1/20,000 H.5.Central
	2		Ditto	
	3	night	Relieved 17/Rl.F. in Left subsector of Right sector	
	4		Quiet.	
	5		Quiet	
En 10 B Chateau des Trois	6		Battn. relieved by 14/Welch Regt. Bn. H.Q. & B Coy (less 1 plat) to Brearpers Chateau des Trois Tours, A Coy to Canal Bank above Nelson Dg, and C Coy Platoons Dawson City, 2 Platoons Anastatt RE FARM; C Coy mess a 17/R.W.F.	
	7		Bequisitions by Coy Officers.	
	8		Working Parties.	
	9		do	
Bivouac 2k	10	Sept	Bn relieved 7/R.W.F. in right subsector of left sector. Patrols under 2nd Lieut Creese to reach N trench ... suppose Snipers post. 2 men wounded.	at C.13.6.9.4.
	11		Quiet.	
	12		Some Machine Gun Fire - otherwise quiet.	29 4 plat
	13		Quiet.	

WAR DIARY or INTELLIGENCE SUMMARY

Army Form C. 2118.

Instructions regarding War Diaries and Intelligence Summaries are contained in F.S. Regs., Part II. and the Staff Manual respectively. Title pages will be prepared in manuscript.

(Erase heading not required.)

Place	Date 1916 Sept.	Hour	Summary of Events and Information	Remarks and references to Appendices
B.H.Q.				Ref: BELGIUM 28.N.W. 1/20,000
Canal Bk.	14.	night	Relieved by 17/R.W.F.	
Chateau 3 Rome			Bn HQ. C Coy A Coy (less 1 Platoon) to Chateau des Tois Rome. D Coy, 3 Platoon to Dawster City 3 Platoon to Lancashire Farm. B Coy + 1 Plat. A Coy to Canal Bank.	B.28.a.72
	15.		Coy. Inspections. Working Parties.	not Crash
	16.		Bn. ~~Grouped~~ relieved by 14/R.W.F. HQrs + A. C and Coys proceed to Camp P.	A.1.S.d. central
Camp P.	17.		B Coy moved to E. Bar K of Capeland worked under Bn of 2nd Earl R. Fatigue Parties working on Housesteadings	
	18.		do.	
	19.		do.	
	~~20~~		Bathing by Coys	
	~~21~~		Coy inspections	
	22	aft.	Inspection by Genl. Plumer, commanding Second Army. do.	
	23.		Coy Parades do.	
	24.		Church Parade. Fatigue Working Parties Cable Laying in front of Canal.	
	25.		Parade. do.	

WAR DIARY or INTELLIGENCE SUMMARY

Army Form C. 2118.

September 1916

Place	Date 1916	Hour	Summary of Events and Information	Remarks and references to Appendices
Pont Oise	Sept.			Map: BELGIUM 2 I/N
Camp P	26		Coy Parade. Night working parties cable laying	1/50,000 A.I.S.L central
	27		do	
	28		do	
	29		do	
	30		do	

Army Form C. 2118.

WAR DIARY
INTELLIGENCE SUMMARY
(Erase heading not required.)

October 1916
16th Welsh

Place	Date 1916	Hour	Summary of Events and Information	Remarks and references to Appendices
Camp P	Oct. 1		Church Parades. Night working parties, cable-laying.	BELGIUM 28nw. 50550 2nd.Divnl.H.
	2	Night	Relieved 13/Welch Regt in left support of Right Sector. H.Qrs. D Coy at Machine Gun Farm. A.B.C Coys on Canal Bank.	A. 15.c.6.9t.ob. 2nd.Divnl.HQ. 2nd.Divnl.
3. Machine Gun F'm	3	Night	Relieved 14/Welch Regt in left sub-sector of Right Sector.	2nd.Divnl. 2nd.Divnl.
	4		Quiet day. At night a German patrol approached the advanced post at head of Motelje Estaminet but were bombed by our post. One German was brought back. He did shortly afterwards. He belonged to 1st Grenadier Guards.	2nd.Divnl. C.15.c.8.5 2nd.Divnl. 2nd.Divnl.
	5		Quiet. Some damage to parapet by enemy artillery.	2nd.Divnl.
	6		Quiet. Front line shelled a little, chiefly in the afternoon, but little damage done.	2nd.Divnl.
	7		Rather more artillery activity than yesterday - Front line shelled - some damage to parapet.	2nd.Divnl.
H.Q. MACHINE GUN FARM	8	Night	Quiet day. Relieved 17/R.W.F. in left support of Right Sector. H.Qrs and D Coy at Machine Gun Farm. B + C Coys on Canal Bank. "A" Coy at Bow Hqrs in the line.	H.S.c.8.9 2nd.Divnl. 2nd.Divnl.
	9		Inspection by Coy Officers - working parties.	2nd.Divnl.
	10		Parade - working parties to front line -	2nd.Divnl.
	11	Night	Battn. relieved 17/R.W.F. in left subsector of Right Sector.	C.20.d.45. 2nd.Divnl.
	12		Major J.R. Angus resumed tempy. Command of Bn. during absence of Lt. Col. F.H.Smith. During	2nd.Divnl.

Army Form C. 2118.

WAR DIARY
INTELLIGENCE SUMMARY.   October 1916
(Erase heading not required.)

Place	Date 1916	Hour	Summary of Events and Information	Remarks and references to Appendices
	Oct. 12		The nightly raids on the German trenches was carried out by 19/reds R.W.F. There was also a raid on our left. Our front line and supports were very heavily shelled in retaliation - much damage done and several casualties.	BELGIUM 28 NW 20000 M Smith M Smith
	13		Quiet day. Raids carried out on the Sectors on our right and left - we were again very heavily shelled in retaliation and much damage done to parapets.	M Smith M Smith M Smith
	※		Lt. Col. Smith resumed command of the Bn. on return from 9th Corps H.Q. Course.	M Smith
	14		Quiet day. Some shelling of front line but no damage done.	M Smith
CHATEAU DES TROIS TOURS	15	night	Relieved 17/R.W.F. in Right Support of Left Sector - H.Qrs, "B" Coy, & A Coy Rear (Iselaton) & Chateau des T Tours, D Coy & Canal Bank. "C" Coy in the line at Lancashire Fm.	B28 a 6¼ M Smith M Smith
	16		Inspection by Coy. Officers - Working parties.	M Smith
	17		Parade - Working parties.	M Smith
	18		do.	M Smith
	19		do.	M Smith
	20		Enemy fired some shrapnel over & Camp at TROIS TOURS between 7 and 9 am.	M Smith
		night	Relieved 17/R.W.F. in Right Sub. Sector of Left Sector. An officers patrol went out to examine the enemy wire about CI&a 17 and lost one O.R. missing.	M Smith M Smith

Army Form C. 2118.

WAR DIARY
or
INTELLIGENCE SUMMARY.
(Erase heading not required.)

October 1916

Instructions regarding War Diaries and Intelligence Summaries are contained in F. S. Regs., Part II. and the Staff Manual respectively. Title pages will be prepared in manuscript.

Place	Date 1916	Hour	Summary of Events and Information	Remarks and references to Appendices
	Oct 20		Quiet.	BELGIUM 28 NW 20,000 2M Smith MSS
	21		Quiet day. Enemy put a number of T.M. shell over our front line in the evening.	2M Smith
	22		Quiet day. Enemy trench mortars active during evening, causing several casualties.	2M Smith
	23		Quiet day. Enemy trench mortars not heal. Must not had to be done training and repairing.	2M Smith
	24		Quiet. - Owing to wet weather, much work had to be done training and repairing.	2M Smith
	25 night		Relieved 13/Welch Regt in Right Reserve, Right Sector. Hqrs & Bn. (also 3 platoons)	C 25 - d 45 2M Smith 2° C°
			to Canal Bank. 2 platoons to IRISH F.M. 1 platoon to FRASCATI F.M.	2M Smith
	26		Coy. Officers Inspections - working Parties	2M Smith
	27		do —	2M Smith
	28		do —	2M Smith
	29		do —	2M Smith
CAMP E	30 night		Bn. Relieved by 13/Welch Regt. and proceeded to Camp E. by tram from YPRES ASYLUM. detraining at BRAND HOEK	A 30 a 60 2M Smith 2M Smith
	31		Coy parade and inspections.	2M Smith

16th Welsh Regt.

Army Form C. 2118.

WAR DIARY
INTELLIGENCE SUMMARY.

November 1916.

Place	Date 1916	Hour	Summary of Events and Information	Remarks and references to Appendices
Camp E	Nov 1		Coy Parades and inspections	Map Loc. A.30.a.6.0
	2		do.	
	3		do.	
	4		Battn. proceeded by train from BRANDHOEK to YPRES ASYLUM, & relieved 13/Welch Regt. (Support Bn. Rt. Subsection Rt. Section) HQ. Canal Bank.	
Ypres Bank	5		Two Platoons to IRISH FARM and one to FRASCATI FARM, under O/c 11/S.W.B.	
	6		Rest on Canal Bank, Dug Outs, Camping R.E. Stores, &c.	
	7		do.	
	8		do.	
Ypres	9		Battn relieved 17/R.W.F. in Left Subsection Right Section (TURCO).	
	10		Quiet. No casualties	
	11		do.	
	12		do.	
	13		do.	
	14		do.	

Army Form C. 2118.

WAR DIARY
INTELLIGENCE SUMMARY.
(Erase heading not required.)

2.

November 1916

Place	Date	Hour	Summary of Events and Information	Remarks and references to Appendices
ROREO	Nov. 15th 1916.		Battn. relieved by 14/Welch Regt. On relief, H.Qrs., B Coy. 2Plat A Coy to CHATEAU des TROIS TOURS, D Coy. to MACHINE GUN Fm, and C Coy. 2 Plat A Coy to CANAL BANK.	
3 TOURS CH.AU	16		Working Parties. Coy. Inspections.	
	17		Raid on High Command Redoubt by in/Yorks Rgt. 20 prisoners in our Lines. Coy. Inspections. in command Rgt. at the number.	
	18		do. do.	
LANC FARM	19		Relieved 17/R.W.F. in LANCASHIRE FARM decto (Rt. Subsector Left Section)	
	20.		Quiet day. No casualties.	
	21.		" One casualty, wounded, at Duty.	
	22		" No casualties	
	23		" "	
	24		" "	
	25		Relieved by 14 R.W.F. 2 Coys. 2 Coys. 1 Coy. 16/R.W.F. 1 Coy. 13/R.W.F. Battn. proceeded by train from YPRES ASYLUM & PSELM. O.E.K to HERNU to Camp 'P'.	
Camp P.	26		Cleaning up. Working Parties.	

H. Ma[...]
Lt Col
O/C 16 Bn RWF

Army Form C. 2118.

WAR DIARY
or
INTELLIGENCE SUMMARY
(Erase heading not required.)

3 November 1916

Place	Date	Hour	Summary of Events and Information	Remarks and references to Appendices
Camp 'P'	1916 Nov 27.		Battn. trained. Raiding Party of 4 Offrs. 120 O.Rs. to Camp 'E' for training. Working Parties.	
	28		Raiding Party to 'E' Camp. Working Party.	
	29		" "	
	30		Corps Commander inspects Brigade at Camp E. & Bosnes presents Military medals to 3 O.Rs. of 14/Worc. Regt. & 1 O.R. of 123 Coy. R.E. Casualties: 1 O.R. of 17/R.W.F. at 115/TMB. to gallantry in connection with raid on HIGH COMMAND REDOUBT.	[signature] C. 11 R.W.F.

WAR DIARY
or
INTELLIGENCE SUMMARY
(Erase heading not required.)

Army Form C. 2118.

Sheet 1.
December 1916
16th WELSH   Vol 13

Place	Date 1916	Hour	Summary of Events and Information	Remarks and references to Appendices
Camp "P"	Dec. 1st		Parades 9am – 12.30pm. Raiding Party training at E Camp under Capt. Russell Jones. Working Parties during day & night.	
	2nd		Parades 9am – 12.30pm. Raiders training at Camp E. Working Parties during day.	
	3rd		Church Parade. Some working parties during the day. Bathing.	
H.Q. Support Bn. R.F.A. River Bks (CANCO)	4th		Battn. entrained at RESELHOEK for YPRES ASYLUM, proceeded thence to quarters on Canal Bank of Left Support Battn., Right Brigade. 14/Welch Regt. in the Line. 17/R.W.F. remaining at Camp G for 4 days.	
	5th		Work on improving Canal Bank. Canal Bks Defences, making Ragbolt frames for dugouts.	
	6th		Night parties on ATLAS TRENCH. Bright moonlight.	
	7th		Same carrying parties also carrying wiring pickets from dumps to front line. Same parties as yesterday also working parties putting up double apron wire at D21. Aus 83 under Lt. HOGARTH & Lt. BOSTOCK respectively. 90 yards erected at D21, and 50 yards at B8. Bright moonlight.	
	~~		Lt.Col. F.W.SMITH proceeded to 115/Inf.Bde. HQrs. to act as Brigadier General during temporary absence of Brig.Genl. A.J. HICKIE. Capt. E.E. KING assumes temporary command of the Battalion.	
	8th		Working parties sow to 25/Division at position 807. Same carryparties. Same carryparties as yesterday.	J.W. Smith Lt Col

Sheet 2

WAR DIARY
or
INTELLIGENCE SUMMARY.
(Erase heading not required.)

Army Form C. 2118.

December 1916

Place	Date 1916	Hour	Summary of Events and Information	Remarks and references to Appendices
Support Bn, TURCO Sect	Decr. 9th		Making + Work on Canal Bank. Fitting Anti Gas Fans to Dugouts. Wiring at D.3.1. P.8. under 2/Lt. BROWNING & Lt. JONES.	
	10th		Shure 20th Sept. Wiring at D.3.1 under 2/Lt. BELL & at P.8. under 2/Lt. TURNBULL. 30 yds & wired at D.3.1 and 25 yds wired at P.8.	
	11th		Battn. relieved by the 13th Bn. Royal Sussex Regt. (116th Brigade, 39th Divn.). On relief proceeded to YPRES ASYLUM & remained for BRANDHOEK and 'E' Camp	
BOESINGHE Front Line	12th		Battn. proceeded by Road to the BOESINGHE sector, & relieved the 4/5th Black Watch in the Line. 10/S.W.B. in support. 3 Coys in the line (A,B,D) 1 Coy (C) in reserve in "C" Line. Belgian Army on our immediate left/ Our line held by 2 Platoons per Coy in the Front ("A") Line, 2 Platoons + Bn HQrs being in the support ("B") Line. Quiet night. No casualties. Under 11th Inf. Bde., 39th Divn.	1/11th Inf Bde Operation order on file
	13th		Enemy Trench Mortars Belgian Area, also our left Coy's Front, breaching the parapet. 2/Lt. T.H. JOHNS & L. S. DAVIES reconnoitred Bridge which was found over the lines at B.12.a.95.75 (Map Belgium 28 N.W.) 1/S.W.B. owing command oppoto Draft of 50 men arrived: 15 to A + D Coys each 9 7/2 to B, C Coys. 2/Lt. B.G.P. wounded	1/S.W.B. own comd oppoto
	14th		Enemy quiet, except for occasional bursts of M.G. Fire. Left (B)'s parapet	E.W. Owitt 2nd Lt.

WAR DIARY
or
INTELLIGENCE SUMMARY.
(Erase heading not required.)

Army Form C. 2118.

Sheet 3

December 1916.

Instructions regarding War Diaries and Intelligence Summaries are contained in F. S. Regs., Part II. and the Staff Manual respectively. Title pages will be prepared in manuscript.

Place	Date 1916	Hour	Summary of Events and Information	Remarks and references to Appendices
BOESINGHE	Decr. 14th.		repaired. Work on front line + communication trenches, also on "B" + "C" Lines and at B.H.Q. Casualties - nil.	
	15th.		Enemy dropped about a dozen 4.2"s in BOESINGHE Village. HUNTER + RAILWAY Trenches blocked in several places. Our Artillery registered during the day. Enemy exposed himself very little, but called frequently to our men. Capt. RUSSELL JONES made a reconnaissance of the enemy front side of the Canal. He left our bank at dark + waded through the Canal, which he found to be about 4 ft. deep of free from wire. He climbed the opposite bank + got to within 4 yards of the enemy parapet where he was stopped by wire. Wire could be cut easily by wire cutters. Enemy could be heard talking + moving about in the Front Line. He came back through the Canal. Work:- Trench Repairs + improvements. Casualties:- nil.	
	16th.		Enemy shelled BOESINGHE Village about 11am with L.H.V. Shells. Between 1 + 3 pm HUNTER TRENCH damaged by T.M's. Enemy M.G's active during night. Work:- Repairing HUNTER TRENCH, wire + other repairs + improvements. Casualties:- nil.	A.W. Smith Lt.
"L" Line	17th.		Battalion relieved 6.40 pm by 10/S.W.B. Bn. HQrs. "D"Coy to M.G.Fm, "C"Coy to BURGOMASTER Fm - L8, A Coy to ELVERDINGHE Defences - L6, B Coy, Coy HQ, + 2 Platoons to L4.	

WAR DIARY
or
INTELLIGENCE SUMMARY.

Army Form C. 2118.
Sheet H.
December 1916.

Place	Date 1916	Hour	Summary of Events and Information	Remarks and references to Appendices
"L" Line	Dec. 17th		and 2 Platoons to McMahon Fm, L2. 11/S.W.B. relieved at these Posts - relief complete 9.20pm. Brig Gen. Hickie returned to Bde. H.Qrs., & Lt.Col. Smith proceeded to VIII Corps. Senior Officers School for a days Comndg. Officers' Course. Capt. King in command.	
	18th		Cleaning up. Work on defences.	
	19th		Bathing. Work on defences. Short parade 8.30am - 9am.	
	20th		Inspections 8.30 - 9 am. Work on defences 9.12.30, 2-4.30 pm.	
	21st		do.	
	22nd		Change in dispositions: Bn. H.Qrs. + 2 Platoons of "C" Coy at M.G. Fm., 1 Plat "B" Coy. + 1 Plat. "D" Coy. at L8, "B" Coy. less 1 Platoon L4, "A" Coy + "D" Coy. less 1 Plat. L6, "C" Coy. less 2 Plat. L2. No 2 Platoon of "C" Coy at M.G. Fm. are billeted there temporarily, pending construction of dugouts at L3 (Brielen) when they will occupy that post. Work on Defences usual hours. 50 men sent from M.G.Fm. to work at L2.	
	23rd		do.	
	24th		Lt.Col. Smith returned from VIII Corps School, & resumed command of the Battn.	
	25th		Christmas Day. No working parties. In addition to usual Rations, £8 of Turkey or Goose supplies to each man (from Divnl. Canteen profits), also Christmas	S.M. Smith

WAR DIARY
or
INTELLIGENCE SUMMARY.
(Erase heading not required.)

Army Form C. 2118.

Sheet 5

December 1916

Place	Date 1916	Hour	Summary of Events and Information	Remarks and references to Appendices
"L" Line	25th		Pudding supplied by "Daily Telegraph" & "Daily News" fund. Work on defences: usual hours.	
	26th		.L4 shelled, one man killed.	
	27th		do.	
	28th		do.	
	29th		All Officers Kits, Blankets, Water Carts &c returned to Transport prior to move on 30th.	
	30th		Transport moved, saw to MERCKEGHEM, arriving at 7pm. Mess Stores and Officers collects by S.S. Wagons + loaded onto a lorry at Brigade Headquarters, ELVERDINGHE CHATEAU. Battalion relieved by 10/Royal Sussex Regt. at 6.30pm. Proceeded independently by Sections to X Road at Gd.d.4.4 (Map: BELGIUM 28NW 20000) where the Battalion assembled. Battn. reported present at 9.30pm. and moved to CHEESEMARKET Station, POPERINGHE, where it entrained (3 trains). Trains moved away about M.N. to BOLLEZEELE, where the Battalion detrained 3am, + proceeded by road to MERCKEGHEM.	
MERCKEGHEM.	31st		Battalion all billeted Ham. Day spent cleaning up, and preparing for training.	
			CASUALTIES:- 1 O.R. Killed. 1 O.R. Wounded.	

16 Bn Welch R.
Sheet 1.   Army Form C. 2118.

WAR DIARY
or
INTELLIGENCE SUMMARY
(Erase heading not required.)

January 1917.   Vol 14

Place	Date	Hour	Summary of Events and Information	Remarks and references to Appendices
MERKEGHEM	1917 Jan 1st		Parades:- Reveille - Cleaning Parade under O.O officers (cult. through Training) Morning 8.45am Parade. P.D. P.T. Coys Arm Drill, Musketry, Str. sear of weaving Parties, Wiring drill. 20 Bombers attacking Bke. Class, fire bays drainage Afternoon (2.30 - 3.30pm daily) Kit Inspection. 2/Lt A.L.JONES appointed Adjutant vice Capt. A.H.L.A. HARRIS (R.A 11.7.16) unit effect from 12.7.16. 2/Lt T.E.S. TUFFIELD Reported. Two Drafts of 20 joined & arrival taken on strength to Batt. B Coy. Parade:- Morning. Physical drill, PD, Btt. Musketry, Extended order drill, wiring. Offensive Gas drill. Afternoon Gas drill. Lectures and instruction Senior Officers Tactical Schemes Inspection by A.D.M.S. of Billets.	
	3rd		Parades:- Morning. P.D. Coys Coy Bn. Drill wiring Drill Bomb Training & Range work. Afternoon. Musketry, Flank Attack by Cos. New Years Honours included M.C. to Lieut M.G. PETTIGREW (RAMC) mentioned in despatches: Lt Col F.W. SMITH and 78230 85 L/Sd D. WILLIAMS. J.R. Angus Major H.	

WAR DIARY
or
INTELLIGENCE SUMMARY

(Erase heading not required.)

Army Form C. 2118.

January 1917

Place	Date	Hour	Summary of Events and Information	Remarks and references to Appendices
MERCKEGHEM	1917 Jany 4th		Parades:- Morning: C.O's Orderly Room, Drill, Company Drill, Bayonet & Lewis Gun drill, training. O.R. room. Coy drill. Lectures on Latrines. Brigade & Army Sports have commenced. Attention is to told Cup Matches in Football (Rugby Rules). Boxing & so on by way of keen sport fighting & bomb throwing. Consolidation of musketry. These competitions will be carried through Units & then on to Bde, Divn, Corps, Army & G.H.Q. Competitions will be opened over the next two or three months.	
	5th		Morning: Bayonet fighting, Lewis gun drill, Platoon attacks, exercise in use of musketry. Afternoon: D Coy at 30 yds Range. Remainder. Bayonet fighting, Musketry. The Divny Commander (General Plumer) inspected the Coys at work during the afternoon & also inspected the lining of R.E. Fiddling in our Pack Mules. He was accompanied by Brig. Genl. Hickie.	

J.B. Angus Major

Army Form C. 2118.

January 1917.

WAR DIARY
or
INTELLIGENCE SUMMARY.

(Erase heading not required.)

Place	Date	Hour	Summary of Events and Information	Remarks and references to Appendices
MERICOURT			Parade. Morning. Musketry. Attack by Coys. on Enemy Trenches. Consolidation. 10/- pm. Outpost drill.	
			Boxing Competition. Game (4 Boys) 20 O.R.s	
			Sunday. Cof E. Church parade on field at BELLEZEELE. Brigade Parade.	
			Afternoon Boxing B. Coy played D. Coy in the Final round of Inner-football Competition. B Coy won 2-1. In afternoon B played D in final (CCoy & DCoy scratched). B Coy won 3-0.	
			Major C. RALPHS returned from 10 months leave to perfect his C.O's A.DEAR NOT arrived and welcomed by Batt.	
			Parade. Morning. Going to sodden condition of Training Area, the road through Area carries; Physical drill. Arms drill by Coys. Boy Drill, Musketry, Bayonet Drill. "A" Coy at the Range. Transport inspected by Adjutant. of 30/Shrop Drains.	
			Afternoon. Bayonet Fighting.	
			In the morning the following officers joined as the Battn. again 10/S.W.B. in the field (Strand)	

J.B. [signature] Major

WAR DIARY
INTELLIGENCE SUMMARY

Army Form C. 2118.

16/Welch Regt.
January 1917

Sheet 4.

Place	Date	Hour	Summary of Events and Information	Remarks and references to Appendices
HEBUTERNE	1917 January 8th		1/ The Boxing Competition:- 23246 Pte A THOMAS (A Coy) Heavy Wt., 16500 A/L/C WATKINS (A Coy) Middle Wgt, 23002 Cpl T MORGAN (H Coy) Welter, 32667 Pte J H JONES (C Coy) Light ""237 Pte T H DAVIES (A Coy) Feather. Winners won by semis to nil. 2/ Company on Cmdg 16/17) R.W.F. in the final for Bde. of Queen's footballs that Bde. Boxing Cup. 3/Lieut C E EYRES (Transport Officer) to hospital sick. 2/Lt C M LLOYD temporary Officer to duties. 2nd Lt H M SALMON to Bde as Intelligence Officer.	
	9th		1/Company drill. Batt. route march with Brigade Band. 2/ Entrained in Motor Buses for ARNEUX. 3/Evening. Fought for Brigade in Boxing Competition fought 16/Welsh Bn. v 2nd A.S.H. M. represented by Pte ATHOMAS, Heavy, beaten L/Cpl D APPLEY Middle, 23172 Sgt WHITE (A Coy) beats Pte J N JONES Light, 40707 Sgt N MANNING (A Coy) Feather. Men turned out. (Pte THOMAS Cook). Bde. Cross Country Championship run off in afternoon won by 16/RIR. Men Ran. out 25th onto.	
	10th		Carabiers Training P.D. 2nd day of photographs taken to Bde attached in afternoon.	

J. Q. Angus Major

Sheet 5.   16/Welch Regt.
        January 1917.

WAR DIARY
or
INTELLIGENCE SUMMARY.

Army Form C. 2118.

(Erase heading not required.)

Instructions regarding War Diaries and Intelligence
Summaries are contained in F. S. Regs., Part II
and the Staff Manual respectively. Title pages
will be prepared in manuscript.

Place	Date 1917 Jany	Hour	Summary of Events and Information	Remarks and references to Appendices
MERKESHEN	10th		Parades(contd) Afternoon. Battn. proceeded to Railway area to Rly Attack in 1½ two rows on either wing to Kampstation. Parades:- Morning. P.D. B.F. Rain storm prevented Parade after 10am. Afternoon. Musketry, rapid loading & aiming. C.O., 2nd in Command, Coy & Coy Commanders inspected arms to be held in Battn under Bde C. port Scheme. Lieut. F.G. NOTTON & E.M. JONES reported their arrival & reported to A & D Coys.	
	11th			
	12th		Parades:- Morning. Too wet for parade. Too bars fitted to Afternoon Rle. Attack. Afternoon. Battn. drew rifles & ammunition & oreas for Brigade attack. Inspected by Brigadier Gel. Gwinn & too wet to carry out attack.	
	13th		Parades:- Morning. P.D. & R.F. Arm. Drill. Rle. handling & Bob Box Repair & Drill. Musketry.	

J.R. Angus Major

Army Form C. 2118.

10th Ulster Regt.

WAR DIARY
or
INTELLIGENCE SUMMARY.
(Erase heading not required.)

January 1917

Place	Date	Hour	Summary of Events and Information	Remarks and references to Appendices
MERCKEGHEM. Camp P.	1917 Jany 13th		Afternoon. Preparation for move to Camp P (POPERINGHE)	
	14th		Batt. (less Transport) moved to POPERINGHE by train from BOLLEZEELE leaving at 8.8am & 9.18am on arrival of Trains at POPERINGHE (MEESEGHEM) Coys. proceeded to Camp P. Transport proceeded by road, leaving BOLLEZEELE under Bde. arrangements at 8 am.	
POPERINGHE	15th		Batt. relieved 11/Royal Sussex Regt (39th Div) at Roussel Farm. Bn. O. R. Boussetleets	
BOESINGHE	16th		Relieved by 1st N. Lanc. Regt. (39th Div.), proceeded to to BOESINGHE acts to relieve 13/Royal Sussex Regt. in the Front Line. Disposition of the Battn:- A Coy on right, B Coy centre, C Coy left, D Coy in support (in BOESINGHE Redoubt & Line) Quiet night. No casualties. Snow. Continued wiring. Day quiet. Observation poor owing to snowfall. During night reconnaissance of R. Yser rendered throw few bombs into Canal. enemy party seen at forward end of BOESINGHE Bridge (unaltered on enemy side previously known) Wiring continued. Work continued on drainage & trench repairs. Annotated.	On our right 113 Inf. Bde. On our left Belfast
	18th		PALL MALL reported a patrol of about 6 A Coy. Enemy artillery & Trench Mortars fairly active during day. Our artillery	

J. R. Angus Major

Army Form C. 2118.

Sheet 7   10th Welch Regt.

WAR DIARY
or
INTELLIGENCE SUMMARY.

January 1917.

(Erase heading not required.)

Instructions regarding War Diaries and Intelligence Summaries are contained in F.S. Regs., Part II. and the Staff Manual respectively. Title pages will be prepared in manuscript.

Place	Date	Hour	Summary of Events and Information	Remarks and references to Appendices
BOESINGHE	18th Jany		retaliated. Casualties Nil. Mining & usual repairs.	
	19th		During day enemy fired several rifle grenades. We replied. Enemy shelled BOESINGHE VILLAGE with 4.2" Shells, also trench mortar Bombs. Our Artillery replied. Machine gunning continued. Casualties Nil.	
	20th		During day enemy artillery & TM's were active; our artillery replied effectively. Batte. relieved by 10/8 W.B. On relief Bn proceeded to BLUET FARM Support Bn.	
BLUET FM			A Coy to EMILE FARM, "C" Coy to the "E" Line, B & D Coys to the X Line. Casualties 3. O.R. wounded. Working parties supplied for R.E.	
	21st		"	
	22nd		"	
	23rd		"	
			Enemy shelled BLUET FM & BOESINGHE ELVERDINGHE Road. Casualties Nil.	
	24th		Weather V. wet & stormy. Ration Parties.	
			The Battn. had to have baths, but owing to water being frozen could not do so. Change of clothing was obtained. Casualties Nil.	
BOESINGHE			Battn. relieved 10/8 W.B. in BOESINGHE & took up dispositions. H. Coy in Lt. C. Coy in centre,	

J.R. [signature]
[signature]

Sheet 8   16/Welch Regt.

WAR DIARY
or
INTELLIGENCE SUMMARY.
(Erase heading not required.)

Army Form C. 2118.

January 1917.

Place	Date 1917	Hour	Summary of Events and Information	Remarks and references to Appendices
BOESINGHE	Jany 24th		D. Coy. left. B. Coy. in Support in BOESINGHE REDOUBT. Night quiet. Casualties nil. Wiring done, but found too hard for pickets owing to look.	
	25th		During the day, enemy Artillery were fairly active near RAILWAY TRENCH & BOESINGHE CHURCH. Our Artillery retaliated. Work on front line, communication trench. Lieut. G.F. DUDLEY (gazetted in the Field 1-17) reported his arrival; posted to A Coy. The night was quiet. Wiring continued. Casualties nil.	
	26th		Day passed quietly; a few rifle grenades were fired by enemy. Quiet night. Canal pumps to keep water open. Wiring continued. Mortal trench repairs and improvements. Casualties — 1 O.R. wounded.	
	27th		During the day the enemy was fairly quiet, he sent over a few rifle grenades, to which we replied. At night he sent over a number of rifle grenades, we again retaliated. Wiring continued, also worked trench drains. Casualties — 3 O.Rs. (1 Officer (2nd Lt T.B. JONES) wounded)	
	28th		Enemy again active with rifle grenades, we replied. Our artillery during	How to
ROUSSEL FM.			Batt. relieved by 11/Sco. B. On relief proceeded to ROUSSEL FARM. Casualties nil.	of Elverdinghe

J.R. Ambrose
Lt Col

Army Form C. 2118.

Sheet 9.

Nofflech Regt.
January 1917.

WAR DIARY
or
INTELLIGENCE SUMMARY.
(Erase heading not required.)

Instructions regarding War Diaries and Intelligence Summaries are contained in F. S. Regs., Part II. and the Staff Manual respectively. Title pages will be prepared in manuscript.

Place	Date	Hour	Summary of Events and Information	Remarks and references to Appendices
Russell in	1917 Jan 29th		Major ANGUS assumed command of the Batt. vice Lt Col SMITH (to England on leave) Capt BRACHER assumed second in command. Working party of 300 O.R.s to work on Railway. Casualties nil	
	30th		Working party as above.	
	31st		do.	
			Casualties for January :- 1 Officer wounded (2Lt. T.B. JONES) 5 O.Rs " 1 O.R. " (accidentally)	

J.E. Angus
Major

2353 Wt. W3544/1454 700,000 5/15 D. D. & L. A.D.S.S./Forms/C. 2118.

Sheet 1.

16/WELCH REGT. — **February 1917.**

Army Form C. 2118.

WAR DIARY
or
INTELLIGENCE SUMMARY.
(Erase heading not required.)

Instructions regarding War Diaries and Intelligence Summaries are contained in F.S. Regs., Part II. and the Staff Manual respectively. Title pages will be prepared in manuscript.

9/M/15

Place	Date	Hour	Summary of Events and Information	Remarks and references to Appendices
ROUSSEL FM.	1917. Feby. 1st.		Moral. Working parts of 300 O.R. for Railway Construction. Capt. R. HAMILTON R.A.M.C. took over duties of M.O. Working parties as above.	Map locations Sheet BELGIUM. 28 NW. 1/20,000. B.13.a.3.c.
	2nd.			
BLEUET FM.	3rd.		Battn. relieved by 11/S.W.B. at ROUSSEL FM. & relieved 17/R.W.F. at BLEUET FM. B Coy in "E" Line, D Coy PARADOU FM. A & C Coys in X Line. Work very difficult owing to Frost. Parties supplied for R.E's & Front Line Bn. "A" Coy Casualties:- 230510 Pte. LANGFORD W.G. (att 115 T.M.B.) 2-2-17. 38119 L/Sgt WILLIAMS.N. B Coy. (att 38/Divl Trench Mortar Bty) 2-2-17. both wounded.	B.10.c.3.3.
	4th.		Church Services held.	
	5th.		Normal Working Parties. Casualties Nil. Frost. Enemy shelled BLEUET FM. area during the evening. Casualties:- 1 O.R. 23369 L/Sgt THOMAS W.C. "B" Coy wounded. Frost.	2/14 6 sheets
BOESINGHE	6th.		Relieved 17/R.W.F. in Front Line BOESINGHE Sector, 8 p.m. Disposition of Bns:- "C" Coy Right, "B" Coy left, "D" Coy Village, "A" Coy BOESINGHE REDOUBT. The 15/R.W.F. were on our right, 3rd Chasseurs à pied on our left.	From B.12.d.85.70 to B.6.a.46 J.M. Smith Lt. Col.

2353. Wt. W2544/1454 700,000 5/15 D.D.&L. A.D.S.S./Forms/C. 2118.

16/Welch Regt.   February 1917

Army Form C. 2118.

WAR DIARY
INTELLIGENCE SUMMARY

Sheet 2.

Place	Date	Hour	Summary of Events and Information	Remarks and references to Appendices
BOESINGHE	1917 Feb. 6th (cont.)	Night	Quiet. Bright moonlight. Casualties - Nil. The S.O.S. signal which has been a single Catherine Rocket up to this date, now changed to a single very light, colour green.	
	7th		During afternoon enemy shelled left Coy front line, also S.I line and HUNTER + BRIDGE STREETS. Our Artillery + light medium trench mortars replied very effectively. During night enemy put over a medium T.M. which fell into a post and wounded 5 O.Rs. (two have died since) Casualties - 5 O.Rs wounded. Enemy active during day with L.H.V Shells in BOESINGHE Village + Chateau area. Our Artillery retaliated. Work still very confined owing to continued frost. A good deal of camouflage done in BRIDGE STREET + near Bn. H.Qtrs. Otherwise quiet. Casualties - Nil.	
	8th		Enemy still active near Cuttow with L.H.V Shells during the day. No damage. He also sent over some Rifle grenades on the Men's line during the afternoon, to which we retaliated in kind. During night this was repeated. 3.2 Gooseberries in creatine's tu'to along on front. Enemy firing continued. Casualties - Nil.	
	9th			

2353   Wt. W2544/1454   700,000   5/15   D. D. & L.   A.D.S.S./Forms/C. 2118.

Sheet 13. 10th Bat. Regt.

WAR DIARY
INTELLIGENCE SUMMARY

February 1917

Army Form C. 2118.

Place	Date 1917	Hour	Summary of Events and Information	Remarks and references to Appendices
BOESINGHE ROUSSEL FM.	Feb. 10th		Quiet day. Relieved by 11/S.W.B. On relief proceeded to ROUSSEL FARM.	B 100.3.3.
	11th		Sunday. Church Parade. No working parties for R.E's, but salvage of trench occupied till by 115th M.G. Coy. & T.M.B. until they were relieved - commenced. 300 men for Railway Construction. All available supplied for salvage work.	
	12th		Working parties as yesterday. 2/Lt. T.G. SILLEM rejoined the Batta. from England after being wounded.	
	13th		Working parties as yesterday.	
"L" LINE	14th		Relieved 10/S.W.B. in L Line defences. B. Coy. C. Coy (less 1 Platoon), at L6 (Boesinghe). A. Coy less 2 Platoons L4, 1 Pl. at Coy L10 (Reigersburg), 1 Plat. A. Coy C. Coy L8 (Burgomaster), D. Coy less 2 Platoons L2 (McMahonFm.), 2 Platoons D. Coy L3 (Brielen) but quartered at Machine Gun Farm. Bn. H.Qrs. Machine Gun Farm.	H5 central
MACHINE GUN FARM	15th		Quiet on defence. Lt. Col. F.W. SMITH returned from leave & resumed command of the Battn. Major J.R. ANGUS resumed secondin Command. German Aeroplane brought down near ELVERDINGHE. Some shells from	

F.W. Smith Lt.Col.

WAR DIARY
or
INTELLIGENCE SUMMARY
(Erase heading not required.)

Army Form C. 2118.

February 1917

Place	Date	Hour	Summary of Events and Information	Remarks and references to Appendices
"I" LINE	15th.		Enemy Anti-aircraft batteries fell at L2, wounded 2/Lt. R.H. HUTCHINGS, CSM REYNOLDS, & a man who only joined the Battn. on the 11th. 2/Lt. HUTCHINGS remained at duty. Usual work on Defences. Thaw commenced.	
	16th.		"	
	17th.		Sunday. Church Services.	
	18th.		Lt. Col. FORSYTH proceeded to Int. Army School for a week's tour of the Army. Major ANGUS assumed command of the Battn. & Capt. BELCHER 2nd in Command. Work on Defences continued daily throughout the week.	
	19th.		2/Lt. T.R. JONES. wounded 27.1.17. returned to Battn. from VIII Corps Rest Station.	
	20th.		Lieut. W.T. FOSTER rejoined Battn. from the U.K. Company rifles firing 30° ranges daily preparatory to entering Coy Musketry Competition.	
	21st.		2/Lt. L.E. KING proceeded to 1/15-1/18 Rbs. H.Div. for attachment as learner.	
	19th.		Capt. KING made a reconnaissance of the Canal at B.12.6.7.0 to ascertain the possibility of a small raid over the ice. He found however that the ice would not bear any weight, that the cracking made such a noise that	

J.W. Smith ?ch?

WAR DIARY
INTELLIGENCE SUMMARY.

16th Welsh Regt. February 1917

Army Form C. 2118.

Place	Date	Hour	Summary of Events and Information	Remarks and references to Appendices
"L" Line	1917 Feb 19th		He could not get across. He related that a silent raid would be impossible until the ice disappeared completely. Sgt G.H.Jones B Coy accom panied Capt KING.	
	21st		2/Lt NEILSON, with 16/15 E.R.BROWN, D Coy, + G.H.JONES, B Coy, tested the ice on the Canal once again, but reported that it was still cracking.	
	22nd		News received that Capt. RUSSELL JONES was invalided S.K. with para typhoid 16-2-17.	
	23rd		Brigade Guard mounted at ELVERDINGHE CHATEAU. A new system has just been started of disinfecting the men's khaki. Their khaki is taken from them at the Baths + taken to a old train which makes unfortunately by V stoked nicks in tunic collar + trouser band. The men's suits are then taken to the Corps Disinfector + sent back the same night.	
	24th			
	25th		Sunday. No work on defences. Church services. In afternoon the Battn played the Black Watch Entrenching Battalion at Association. Latter Battn held an unbeaten	

J.M.Omith Lt.Col.

16th Welch Regt   February 1917.   Army Form C. 2118.

WAR DIARY
or
INTELLIGENCE SUMMARY.
(Erase heading not required.)

Place	Date	Hour	Summary of Events and Information	Remarks and references to Appendices
2" Line	1917 Feby. 25th	cont	N.Co (?) that were beaten by our XI Coy S.O. The outstanding Players were Q.M.S. HAMLYN (B Coy) + A. GARDINER (D Coy) 28764, the latter scoring 4 goals. Lt. Col. F.W. SMITH returned from 2nd Army School mounted. Amour of Bath. Major ANGUS ascended in Command, proceeded to ELVERDINGHE as Assistant Commandant of ELVERDINGHE Defences.	
	26th		Following Complaint received from Artillery that LAPH our Coys that our men were destroying Tanks for firewood. The C.O. + Adjutant visited an Artillery Billet + interviewed of machine gun Farm + found the whole of this Battery who made the complaint actually burning down logs! Nothing to report.	
	27th 28th		B Coy shot C Coy + A Coy shot D Coy in Musketry Competitions. 30 rounds 25 rounds slow tuition, 5 rounds Loading, 5 rounds Snapshooting + 15 rounds Rapid. C Coy beat B Coy, and A Coy beat D Coy. Capt. F.A. RUSSELL struck off Establishment 10-2-17.	

F.W. Smith Lt Col

March 1917. Sheet 1. 10/Welch Regt.

WAR DIARY
or
INTELLIGENCE SUMMARY.
(Erase heading not required.)

Army Form C. 2118.

Vol 16

Place	Date	Hour	Summary of Events and Information	Remarks and references to Appendices
L Line	1917 March 1st		St. David's Day. In the morning the Final of Musketry Competition was shot off. C Coy beat A Coy. In afternoon Battn. played 115/T.M.B. at Association, and won 4-1. In evening B & C Coys. held a concert at	
	2nd.		ELVERDINGHE. Relieved by 11/SWB in L Line Defences, and relieved 10/SWB at	
BLEUET FARM	3rd.		BLEUET FARM. Disposition:- B & C Coys X Line, A Coy EMILE Fm, D Coy PARADOU Fm. Divisional Rugby Team played Anzacs at BAILLEUL, won. Usual R.E. Wiring Parties nightly while in support.	
	4th.		Capt. T.O. JONES, & Capt. T.H.N. WILLIAMS struck off Establishment of Battn. with effect from 26.2.17	96 /15
	5th		Quiet day. Very cold weather.	
	6th		Relieved by 17/R.W.F. at BLEUET FARM, and relieved 10/SWB in Line, BOESINGHE SECTOR. 2nd Regt. of Carabiniers (6th Belgian Division) on Left, 15/R.W.F. on Left. Battn. Disposition, A Coy right front Line, D Coy Left front line, B Coy Village Street, C Coy BOESINGHE REDOUBT.	?Left
BOESINGHE			Very cold. Moonlight. Quiet night	

T2134. Wt. W708—776. 500090. 4/15. Sir J. C. & S.

Sheet 2. 16/Welch Regt. Army Form C. 2118.

March 1917.

WAR DIARY
or
INTELLIGENCE SUMMARY.
(Erase heading not required.)

Place	Date 1917 March	Hour	Summary of Events and Information	Remarks and references to Appendices
BOESINGHE	7th		Liaison made with the 2d. Cashiers (Capt. PAIROUX) who came to lunch. Brig. Genl. A.J. HICKIE left 115/Inf.Bde. for England. Lt. Col. F.N. SMITH proceeded to Brigade as acting Brig. Genl. Major J.R. ANGUS assumed command of Battn. Quiet at dawn. Very cold. Some snow. Work:- wiring, construction of gates at end of posts.	
	8th		Quiet; moonlight, a stray shot caught two O.Rs. who were wiring on No. 2 Post (A Coy.); both to F.A.	
	9th		VIII Corps Intelligence Officer visited the Line at dawn, & vainly tried to induce the Hun to talk to him. Brig. Genl. J.R. MINSHULL-FORD, D.S.O., M.C., arrived to command 115/Inf.Bde. came to Bn. H.Q. Lt. Col. F.W. SMITH returned to the Battn. Strafe (???) by Heavies on Steam Mill; front line cleared from 3.15–6 p.m. Good wiring of posts done during night. L.Cpl. SERVICE killed. Relieved by 17/R.W.F. in Front Line; on relief Battn.H.Q., A, B & D Coys proceeded to X Camp, C Coy to ROUSSEL FARM.	
X Camp	10th			
	11th		Sunday. Church Parade. Brig. Genl. visited the Camp during afternoon.	J.N. Smith Lt.

March 1917.   Sheet 3.   1/6 Welch Regt

WAR DIARY or INTELLIGENCE SUMMARY

Army Form C. 2118.

Place	Date 1917	Hour	Summary of Events and Information	Remarks and references to Appendices
X Camp	March 12th		Working party of 250 men daily on cable burying. Wet morning. Coys paraded in afternoon for bombing, Lewis Gun instruction musketry.	
	13th		Batt. parade in morning, 9am-/10am. Coy & Platoon drill. March Past with Band 12.Noon. Coy Parades 2-4pm. Capt. F. BIRD struck off establishment, with effect from 2nd Feby. 1917.	
BLEUET FM	14th		Relieved 10/S.W.B. at BLEUET FM. Relief complete 8.45pm. Disposition Battns BLEUET FM., A&D Coys X Line, B Coy PARADOO FM, C Coy MARIE JEANNE FARM.	
	15th		Working parties on repairs on area of the R.E.'s Capt A.M.R. PIRIE R.A.M.C. relieved Capt. HAMILTON R.A.M.C. as M.O. of Batt.	
	16th		Lieut. Rugby Jean May, N.Z. Trench Team. lost by 18.7. 2/Lt. NEILSON, Sgt E.T. BROWN & 6 men set out from C.7.c.00.95 (BELGIUM 28 N.W. 50,000) to endeavour to enter enemy lines at C.7.c.00.95 & obtain identification. They reached the spot where they intended to enter, found a considerable amount of wire existing. The party set out through 3 Knife Rests, when they were opposed by the enemy, who fired. Sgt BROWN was slightly wounded (remained at duty.) Party had to retire, at its being out for over 3 hours.	
	17th		Quiet day. Usual work supplying parties. Beautiful weather.	

S.W. Smith Lt Col

March 1917. Sheet 4. 16/Welch Regt.

Army Form C. 2118.

WAR DIARY
INTELLIGENCE SUMMARY.
(Erase heading not required.)

Place	Date	Hour	Summary of Events and Information	Remarks and references to Appendices.
BLEUET Fm BOESINGHE	1917 March 18th.		Fine weather continued. Relieved the 10/Glosters in the Front line BOESINGHE Sector. Disposition of the Battalion. C Coy Right Coy Front Line, B Coy Left Coy Front line, A Coy. Village Street, D Coy BOESINGHE REDOUBT. 2 Carabiniers on left, 1st R.W.F. on right.	
	19th		Major LETEVRE & Capt PARDOEN of 1st Carabiniers called at B. H.Q. there taken round the line (1st Carabiniers relieving 2nd Cara.b on 26th). O/C B, C & D Coys visited Belgian Lines. 2/Lt NEILSON & his party made another attempt to enter enemy lines. They started again from C.7.0.0.7. & made for the same spot - C.7.a.0.95. They found that someone was busily had been placed behind the one they had cut, & there was also a great deal of loose wire between them & their objective. They cut through the loose wire, through one knife rest & part of another. They could see that there still remained a great deal of loose wire to cut behind the Knife rests, & as the patrol had been out for 4½ hours 2/Lt NEILSON decided to withdraw. Immediately opposite the spot where they were working, a sentry was heard coughing from time to time, & on one occasion a loyal voice was heard to say in good English "bring me a light"	

Sheet 5. 16/Welch Regt. Army Form C. 2118.

WAR DIARY
INTELLIGENCE SUMMARY
(Erase heading not required.)

March 1917.

Place	Date 1917 March	Hour	Summary of Events and Information	Remarks and references to Appendices
BOESINGHE	20th		Major E. COLINET & Capt E. AMEYE of 1st. Carabiniers (3rd Bn. 17/Bde. 6/Belgian Division) called at Bn.H.Q. were taken round the Line. The 10/S.W.B. & 17/R.W.F. proceeded to occupy the centre section of the Divisional Front. 113/Inf.Bde. going back to BOLLEZEELE Area.	
	21st		2/Lt. T.B. JONES, 1st GILBERT & 6.O.R. set out from our Front line at 8.6.c.5.2. at 8.15pm to ascertain the possibilities of wading the YSER CANAL opposite that point with a small wading party. It was found that the bed of the Canal was composed of very soft mud which, at a distance of 8/10yds from the edge, reached to the waist, & it is known to have been for a depth which the patrol had taken. They could not have pulled themselves from the mud. The patrol returned at 8.45pm. They must have been spotted by the enemy, as a grenade was thrown just as the last man of the patrol reached our bank.	
	22nd		None known. Quiet in the Line.	
BLEUET FM	23rd		Relieved by 11/S.W.B. in Front Line. On relief proceeded to BLEUET FARM. Disposition:- Bn. C Coy. X Line, A Coy. PARADOU FARM, D Coy. MARIE JEANNE FM. 25 men of recent draft were brought to PARADOU Fm. for training in Musketry and	

2353 Wt. W.2544/1454 700,000 5/15 D.D.& L. A.D.S.S./Forms/C. 2118.

Sheet 6. 16/Welch Regt.

WAR DIARY
INTELLIGENCE SUMMARY

March 1917.

Place	Date 1917 March	Hour	Summary of Events and Information	Remarks and references to Appendices
BLEUET FM.	23rd		Wiring. Also 6 men per Coy. for Lewis Gun instruction.	
	24th		Training of above men continued. Summer time came into force at 11p.m.	
	25th		Above men wired 40 yards apron on E side of BRIDGE ST (near jct. with X Line) & 60 yards half apron on W side. Belgians raided Germans near STEENSTRAAT (across bridge over Canal) killed many Huns & took six prisoners.	
BOESINGHE	26th		Relieved the 11/S.W.B. in the Front Line BOESINGHE Sect. Disposition of Bn. A Coy. night Coy. Front Line. D Coy. Left Coy. Front Line. C Coy. Village Street. B Coy. BOESINGHE REDOUBT. 10/S.W.B. on right. 1st Cardinians on Left. Relief completed 6.30 p.m.	
	27th		Quiet night.	
	28th		Quiet 24 hrs. Nothing to note.	
	29th		do. One of our 9.45" Mortars fired on German support trenches during afternoon. Germans retaliated, & put a very large number of minnies, rum jars & pine-apple bombs on to Front Line CARDIFF STREET area. Right Coy. Front Line badly damaged in 2 places. Left Coy. Line hit in one place, and one man (Pte. G. BRYANT)	

EM Dmitt
Lt Col

March 1917 Sheet 1. 10/Welch Regt.

Army Form C. 2118.

WAR DIARY
INTELLIGENCE SUMMARY.

Place	Date 1917 March	Hour	Summary of Events and Information	Remarks and references to Appendices
BOESINGHE	29th(th)		killed, and three others wounded. Quiet night.	
	30th.		Relieved by 11/S.W.B. in front line. On relief proceeded to BLEUET FARM; disposition of Coys. D & A Coys X Line, C Coy PARADOU FARM, B Coy MARIE JEANNE FARM.	
	31st.		A draft which arrived at B.H.Q. on 24th were sent to Transport lines under 2/Lt A.O. JONES & 2 NCOs for training in wiring, musketry &c. They were brought back today; tonight they did 1st wiring.	
			Casualties for month :- 2 ORs killed. 5 " wounded.	

J Smith Lee

April 1917.

16/Welsh Regt.

Vol 17

WAR DIARY
or
INTELLIGENCE SUMMARY.
(Erase heading not required.)

Army Form C. 2118.

Place	Date 1917	Hour	Summary of Events and Information	Remarks and references to Appendices
BLEUET FARM	April 1st		Quiet day: usual working parties	
	2nd.		Following promotions appeared in London Gazette 29.3.17:-	
			Temp. Lieuts. to be Temp. Capts:- N.T. RICHARDS 11.2.17, H. Ll. JONES 27.2.17, N.T. FOSTER 27.2.17 } Pro. Os.	
			(2nd Lieut 4)	
			" " Lieuts:- A.W.TAYLOR 11.2.17, F.R.J. BELL 27.2.17, R.H. HUTCHINGS 27.2.17 } 30.05.03	
			" 2nd. " "	73
BOESINGHE	3rd.		Battalion relieved 11/S.W.B. in Front Line BOESINGHE Sector. Relief complete 10.30pm. Moonlight.	
			Disposition:- C Coy right Coy, B Coy left Coy, D Coy VILLAGE St, A Coy REDOUBT. Moonlight.	
	4th.		Snow again: bitterly cold day: very quiet	
	5th.		Snd.Lt. 3303 Sgt. T.Z. MORGAN (A Coy) wounded while wiring.	
	6th.		Good Friday: celebrated by a good deal of mutual trench Mortar attention	
BLEUET FM	7th.		Relieved by 11/S.W.B. Relief complete 10.15 a.m. Proceeded to BLEUET FM (BHQ) } P. Orders	
			C + B Coys X Line, D Coy PARADOU FARM, A Coy MARIE JEANNE FARM. } 1 Sect.	
	8th.		Quiet day, very cold. Working parties daily.	
	9th.		Easter Monday. Snow: great news of pushed ARRAS	
	10th.		Very cold, more snow. Further good trusts of near [illegible] the pusherh 6	
	11th.		interest in G.H.Q. Telegrams	Jw [illegible] Lt Col
			Much good working done & [illegible] by new draft men. The system of keeping	[illegible] 16

WAR DIARY or INTELLIGENCE SUMMARY

Army Form C. 2118.

April 1917. Sheet 2. 10/Welch Reg.

Place	Date 1917 April	Hour	Summary of Events and Information	Remarks and references to Appendices
BLUET FARM	11th		The latest drafts together near Bn. H.Q. where in order to acclimatize in winter fatigues were very beneficial.	
	12th		A new draft of 31 men all from the Essex Regt. into the exception of one who returned to the Bath after being wounded arrived. Good physiques.	En Ordres 88
ROESINGHE	13th		Bn. relieved 11/S.W.B. in front line ROESINGHE Sectr. Disposition HQs, Right D Coy, Left front line, B Coy village street, C Coy Regnt. Sm'l Right.	0.08/25.
	14th		Quiet. Some M.G. fire at night 2nd/Lt. R.E. ELLARD killed whilst running. Major T. LLOYD joined Bn. from 6/T.R.B. 2nd/Lt. A.E.S. D. Coy for direction.	} 3.05 Sec.
	15th		Usual work. Distribution of Commd. Sig. HQ in charge of ROESINGHE Elyard /S.W. Ry/ VIVIAN STREET Bn. mined. 2nd/Lt. T.B. JONES made careful reconnaissance of Front Line. Things at 6 & 7/8.6 + (Left Coy front line) & a certain possibility of enemy to cross the canal? Seen. It was merely a part of rather an open space a shell crater from the bank. Quiet + D.W. Rounds.	
	16th		Quiet. Nothing to note.	
	17th		Major V.R. ANGUS succeeded to attend 3rd Army VIII Corps School. Capt. F.W. BRACHER acting dubton a gleggo in Comnd. Bn. and M. INSHULL FORD attended VIII Corps School course. Draft arrived and taken on strength consisting of man mostly of the Bath.	} 7.B.0. } F. Williams J.W. O'Neil

2353 Wt. W2544/1454 700,000 5/15 D, D. & L. A.D.S.S./Forms/C. 2118.

WAR DIARY / INTELLIGENCE SUMMARY

Army Form C. 2118.

April 1917

Place	Date	Hour	Summary of Events and Information	Remarks and references to Appendices
BOESINGHE	17th		2 men (2735 L/Cpl. C. NELSON & 21404 Pte. E. SHEPPARD) who were reported missing in a raid made on 15.7.16 + attack in MONSTZ ROAD 11.7. Boesinghe, now officially reported as K.I.A. o having died. 25 men of Essex Regt. left, joined Batt.	S. in O.s 87
	18th		Quiet day. Band.	
	19th		Batt. was relieved by 10/8 208 on relief proceeded to X Camp. Experiment of carrying the men like was very successful, but showed need of careful supervision to prevent mixing of Coys. etc. The Batt. now leaves the line area for the first time for 3 weeks.	O.O. Tab.
"X" Camp	20th		Day was spent in cleaning up, and reorganising Coys on the new platoon basis. X Camp is the finest ever occupied by the Batt. With the form of a hollow square, with a Head in the square, adjoining the Camp is a recreation ground which is also used as a football ground. If was a Bath House for which 1500 gallons of water can be obtained from the pond by pumping. 350 men were Enclosure 1. at VIII Corps Divisional R. Every article of clothing also	Appendix 1

S.W. Smith
[signature]

April 1917 16/Welch Regt.

WAR DIARY
INTELLIGENCE SUMMARY

Army Form C. 2118.

Place	Date	Hour	Summary of Events and Information	Remarks and references to Appendices
X Camp Pt E	1917		Blankets disinfected. Remainder, except working parties, have (daily) training according to programme. Range Parade.	Prog of Trg No 2
			Cyclist for at Coast in evening, return 1 a.m.	
	22nd		Xmas Day. Church Parade. 300 men delivered Football in afternoon. Military Catholics normal.	B.O. 91. P. of T.S. 3
	23rd		Major T.R. ANGUS returned from tour (after school) of programme. Training acc'd'g to programme. Weather very bad & wet. Very little improvement noticeable in appearance of men on parade; the battle readies in mud at 9am, & pm. Daily bands playing turnouts. All bugle calls at Hours, + everything has the appearance of being complete. Platoon competition at each other for showing smartest turnouts.	
			Raining	P of T re 4
	24th		Evening Headquarters played "C" Coy in Football, won.	
	29th		Training in afternoon. "C" Coy Sig of War team beat a Coy of 9th CC's.	P of T g 2
			in first Round of competition.	W McNeill Lt Col

April 1917.   Officer's   16 Welch Regt.   Army Form C. 2118.

WAR DIARY
INTELLIGENCE SUMMARY.

Place	Date	Hour	Summary of Events and Information	Remarks and references to Appendices
X Camp	April 26th		Training. Coy Football Matches in evening. Following extracts from "Appointments Commissions":— 2/Lieut. R.H. HUTCHINGS (from 31.1.17) to back Capt while serving as Coy. 2/Lt. J.O. JONES (2.3.17 to 31.3.17)	Ref. T.N.º 6 2 Orr Nº 93 Ref T.Nº 2 P. of T Nº 8
	27th		Coy made in good & platoon in Outpost Scheme. Training in morning. In afternoon to Players 8/17 Northumberlands "E" Coy. 16 of Wear Beaw won the final. match. Coy of 16/17 R.W.F. & 2 wit 4.7.	
	28th		In Divl Church Service on Parade Ground attended by every officer, N.C.O. & Man available. In afternoon Association Foot Ball. A Coy at Adams won 3-0	
	29th		Training.	Ref T Nº 29
	30th		During the whole period a Boxing Ring to have well patterned, good interest being shown & the team which will represent the Brigade in Divl Semi finals on May 1st is in good form.	

J. W. Willis
Lt. Col. |

WAR DIARY or INTELLIGENCE SUMMARY

Army Form C. 2118.

10/Welch Reg.t Vol 18

May 1917 Sheet 1.

Place	Date	Hour	Summary of Events and Information	Remarks and references to Appendices
MERCKEGHEM	1917 May 1st		Batt.n moved to MERCKEGHEM. Left BRANDHOEK Station 5pm, reached ESQUELBECQ 7.10pm, & proceeded from there by Route march.	
	2nd		Batt.n Boxing team won the Divisional Competition, allowed toy not tie 10/Welch Reg.t as a won all rounds. The team consisted of 3259 Sgt. J. DOHERTY, heavy weight, 56500 Cpl W. AEFLEY middle weight, 32667/32. T.W. JONES middle weight, 23172 Sgt. T. WHITE light lover sg.t 23033 Pte. E. BIRD bantam weight	
	3rd		Bay.onet getting every thing ready for training. Another splendid training as according to programme.	
	4th		" do —	Ref. T. No. 1
	5th		The Brigadier General has attened Inter-Coy & Inter-Brigade Coy. Assoc.n football Competitions. "D" Coy played and beat "A" Coy. a Coy "D" won test. "C" Coy in own test. In afternoon A met B Coy at Soccer & B Coy won	" 2.
	6th		Training was a draw of the playing extra time. Sunday – Massed Brigade Church Parade on training Area	" 3.
	7th		In afternoon A & B Coy's played. B Coy won Training	£17 23 sheet " 4. L.G. Angus Capt.n

WAR DIARY
or
INTELLIGENCE SUMMARY

Army Form C. 2118.

(Erase heading not required.)

Place	Date	Hour	Summary of Events and Information	Remarks and references to Appendices
MERKEGHEM	1917 Nov 8th		Training	Ref T.5
	9th		Training Five went on continued	Swim 10.0. N°A
			In the evening B.O Coy went to decide who should represent the Battalion in the Brigade's Competition. The result was as follows:	
			A — Strike Nine and less played	
	13th		Training. As the ground of the Coys in Competition to be played to-morrow B & D Coys decided to go in order to decide which round.	S Raft T.7 9.05. N.N.B
			Tournament B & D Coys decided to go in order to decide which round. In the event B Coy won, the score being 1-0	
	11th		Training. Bathing.	Ref T.8
			In the evening B Coy played C Coy. F.K+F won 2-0	
	12th		Training. Battalion attended, watched by the Army Commander. Aeroplane contest won very successful.	Ref T.9 10.0. N.O. C
			General Luidereon Dinner, B & D went to MEERVOORDE & May to 28th Squadron R.F.C H.Q.	
	13th		Peaceful Sunday, two Church Parades. In the afternoon Brigade Sports were held with Training	

J.G. Anonymous

Army Form C. 2118.

Pl. of 8

1/4 Welch Regt.

WAR DIARY
or
INTELLIGENCE SUMMARY.
(Erase heading not required.)

May 1918.

Place	Date	Hour	Summary of Events and Information	Remarks and references to Appendices
	May			
MERRIS (Camp)	13th (cont)		Training. Rugs during the afternoon, the Battalion secured four (4) and six (6) goals	
	14th		Training & six ads. Rugby team beat 17/RWF 28-0.	L. of T. 14.
			"C" Coy won match. The Batt: Whist Drive "beat the winning Coy"	
			17/RWF 10/580 B. replied to the Divisional Final	Bn. O.s 110
			"B" Coy 1. won and 17/RWF Coy. in the Final for the "Bde's"	
			Cup - drew 6-0. The Coys rep play the "Cant Cup" Final	Bn. O.s
			in civies - baggy trous: etc.	
			The Rugby team beat 10/580 B. RWF. 24-6. J. nour replacement	
			drawn in the Divisional Finals.	
	15th		Place holiday	
HERZEELE	16th		Battalion proceeded by Rout March to HERZEELE and remarked	O.Os. 128
	17th			
	18th		There until 18th when it proceeded to one's HOUTKERQUE and	O.Os. 129
Camp	18th		[illegible stamp text] INSULTED FORTEVR at Cam. Major TRANS scommd Bn with MAJOR (LLOYD) 2nd in Command	
WATOU E L Coy 8			On arrival there a wire was received that C Coy	
	18th		Proceed to the Divisional Musketry Competition with a score of 1270 points. Bn. Os 144.	
			The Section was Dur 11.0 am	
BOESINGHE	19th		The Battalion moved from L Camp to the Front Line a BOESINGHE Section relieving	O.Os 130

J.S. Angare
Major

May 1917 10/Welch Regt. Army Form C. 2118.

WAR DIARY
or
INTELLIGENCE SUMMARY
(Erase heading not required.)

Place	Date	Hour	Summary of Events and Information	Remarks and references to Appendices
ROESINGHE	May 1917		10/Welsh Regt. The disposition of the Battn. was: A Coy Right Coy, B Coy Left Coy, A Coy VILLAGE Coy, D Coy REDUCT. The night was very quiet. Considerable Artillery activity our back areas receiving a good deal of attention. The front line was very quiet, during the night not a single M.G. bullet or rifle grenade of any description was fired. Casualties nil.	
	20th		Quiet. A little hostile Artillery fire on VILLAGE & RAILWAY STREETS during the morning. Hostile Trench Mortars active throughout the day. If it were not for the Very lights one would be another quiet day. This we believe that the enemy front line is empty.	Casualties 1 OR wounded A.0.116.
	22nd		A very strange occurrence. Found to-day No 55340 Pte J.W. COOPER was found wounded in a small shellhole behind our front line. On questioning him from what could be gathered he said was medical evidence that the soldier ( ) suffered severe from wounds in no way in the Battalions experience.	B.O.145
	23rd		A Coy relieved by 10th R.W.F. these relief fell behind VILLAGE STREET and one officer killed & wounded 2330 x C.S.M. GOODWIN A) and wounded 8, one at duty	
	24		Quiet day very little shelling 2 O.R. wounded at duty	

J.B. Ingram
Major

16 Welch Regt.

Army Form C. 2118.

May 1917

WAR DIARY
or
INTELLIGENCE SUMMARY.
(Erase heading not required.)

Place	Date	Hour	Summary of Events and Information	Remarks and references to Appendices
BOESINGHE	May 25th		Relieved by 11 S.W.B. On relief by the Brigade at St BLEUET FARM, B Coy PARADOX Fm, C Coy MARIE JEANNE Fm, & A & D Coys X lines.	O.O. 131
BLEUET Fm			The unsuitable thing about the last period in the front line was the total absence of M.G. & T.M. fire. This afternoon the Heavy T.M. firing 29 of fired 20 of the Heavy Trench Mortar while the Lieutenant fired over 2/3000 rounds. Did not one round was sent back to ordination.	
	26th		Quiet day. Some working parties to front daily under Pioneer supervision. The weather is beautiful & the trees are in BLEUET Farm look splendid.	
	27th		Whit Sunday. A terrifying a walk talk of 1.0 of 9.7 O.O. under A.O. moves about us. B to be to the Boche & one was made by 72k & passing by the Hun was a little over a hundred yards behind our left. The owe tank so the project was reported.	
	28th		At 2.30am we took up on Gen. Alarm which came from the right. It turned known to be a false of alarm.	
			The following from one T.M.s apprised in the Orders of the day	30.5.17
				J.B. Angus Major

Sheet 6.

Welch Regt.

May 1917.

WAR DIARY
INTELLIGENCE SUMMARY

Army Form C. 2118.

Place	Date	Hour	Summary of Events and Information	Remarks and references to Appendices
BLEUET FARM	May 1917 28th		To be Acting Major :- Capt. H.P. HERODIAN dated 9.3.17	
			Captain :- Lieut. A. MESSITT " 9.3.17	
			Lieut :- 2/Lieut. J. M. C. LEWIS " 9.3.17 ⎫ London Gazette 22.5.16	
			2/Lieut. H. M. SALMON " 19.3.17 ⎬	
			T/2/Lieut D. G. BOSTOCK " 16.3.17 ⎭	
	29th		Lt. Col. F.W. SMITH assumed command of the Bn. (from Bde.) & Major	
			J.R. ANGUS resumed duties as second in command.	
			The Field Marshal C. HAIG's despatch the following Officers + NCOs of this	
			Bn. are now mentioned :-	
			Lieut. Col. F.W. SMITH	
			Major J.R. ANGUS	
			23088 Sgt. D. WILLIAMS	
			Has received flag 23088 Sgt. D. Williams has a ... the	
			Croix de Guerre.	
	30th		The Battn. was billetted in huts of about 40 feet & took over ... in Trench	
			ROTHERHAM TRENCH & the depth of about 1/2 about the ... complete in fight.	
				J.B. Angus Major

Sheet N°1. 16/Welch Regt. May 1917. Army Form C. 2118.

WAR DIARY
or
INTELLIGENCE SUMMARY.

Place	Date	Hour	Summary of Events and Information	Remarks and references to Appendices
BLEUET Fm.	1917 May 31st		Our Artillery Burst Rates (Heavy Trench Mortars) practice have carried out Annual shoots lately. To-day the 121 Brigade R.F.A. (less "A"D/121) 122 Brigade R.F.A. and 184 Bg/Bn in carried out 20 minutes Practice Barrage on CADDIE TRENCH (KEEL OUT) C.7.8.75.10 — C.7.b.15.70 (Map ST JULIEN 1/10000) and CADDIE SUPPORT RESERVE C.8.6.1825 — 07.6.6025.	
			Bn. relieved 11/SWB in Front Line BOESINGHE SECTION. Relief complete	
		11.15 pm.	Disposition of Battn:-	
			A Coy Right Coy Front Line. D Coy Left Coy Front Line	
			C " VILLAGE Coy. B " REDOUBT Coy.	
			Capt M McKENNA, O.E., is among the Chaplains mentioned in	
			Sir D Kendall Sir Douglas HAIGS Despatch	

L R Knight?
Lt Col
16/Welch

Army Form C. 2118.

16Bn WELCH REGT.
Vol 19

WAR DIARY
or
INTELLIGENCE SUMMARY.

Place	Date	Hour	Summary of Events and Information	Remarks and references to Appendices
BOESINGHE	1917 June 1		REF. Sheet 28. N.W. BOESINGHE SECTION. Disposition of Companies as follows:— Front line (right) "A" Coy Front line (left) D Coy. Reserve Coy village street "C" Coy Reserve Coy Chateau Wood "B" Coy. The day was fairly quiet — during the afternoon a few 10.5 cm How. shells were fired into the village. The night was quiet. Usual maintenance work — 1 Company improving ROTHERHAM ROAD. Major J.R. Angus assumed command of the Batt. vice Lt Col F.W. Smith who proceeded on leave to U.K. Major J.C. Lloyd assumed duties of Second in Command. Casualties O.R. killed 1 wounded 1	20 sheets
	2		Little activity during the morning — during the afternoon our T.M's and artillery carried out a shoot on enemy frontline doing small damage. There was no immediate retaliation but between 6.30 - 7.0 p.m. enemy shelled the village firing heavily doing some damage. Capt. H.H. Jones (App) was wounded by a splinte on Bn. Hq. During the night 1st Canadian Dragoons took to enemy front line with Rifle Grenades and Lewis Guns —	

Army Form C. 2118.

16 WELCH REGT

WAR DIARY
or
INTELLIGENCE SUMMARY.
(Erase heading not required.)

Instructions regarding War Diaries and Intelligence Summaries are contained in F.S. Regs., Part II. and the Staff Manual respectively. Title pages will be prepared in manuscript.

Place	Date	Hour	Summary of Events and Information	Remarks and references to Appendices
BOESINGHE	1917 June 2		Casualties Wounded Officer 1 Capt. WH Jones. O.R. 2. Between 9.30–9.30am the enemy barraged the road between WHITE HOPE CORNER and "X" line – and between 2–2.30pm Shelled BOESINGHE with 10.5cm Howt Battery. BRIDGE ST in several places. A practice barrage was carried out on Brigade front on our right away in the afternoon – there was no retaliation. He fired 1 enemy/post due with rifle grenades and trench mortars during the night. Usual maintenance work carried out to ROTTERDAM ROAD. Casualties Nil.	
	" 3			
	" 4		A gas alarm was heard on our right about 12.30am and was then up on our front – attacks started to respond to on our Rear. The presence of gas was very apparent – it relieved some drifting over from a gas shell bombardment by the enemy near YPRES. Between 5.0–6.0am a heavy barrage was opened in to Brigade on our right. We fired 60/70 rifle grenades into enemy front line between 6.0am – between 9.15–9.30 pm enemy burst about 30 rounds of Heavy HE Shrapnel over	

2353   Wt. W2544/1454 700,000 5/15   D.D. & L.   A.D.S.S./Forms/C. 2118.

Army Form C. 2118.

WAR DIARY
or
INTELLIGENCE SUMMARY.
(Erase heading not required.)

16 WELCH REGT

(3)

Place	Date	Hour	Summary of Events and Information	Remarks and references to Appendices
BOESINGHE	1917 June 4		BRIGADE ST and TRAMWAYS. The enemy's harassing fire on his front line during the night not appreciably as a hour fire. Casualties Nil.	
	5		BOESINGHE Shelled intermittently during the day — Our artillery carried out a practice barrage in the section on our right, taken there was no retaliation — have working parties alright. Casualties Nil	
	6		At 12.30 a.m. in accordance with pre-arranged scheme, two parties respectively led by 2/Lt A.O. Jones and 2/Lt J.O. Jones "B" Coy raided the enemy trenches across the Canal at BOESINGHE. A special roll "mat" was used to cross the Canal (to prevent the raiders sinking into the mud which is very deep) — The left party under 2/Lt A.O. Jones was extraordinarily successful — as they crossed the Canal, entered and searched the enemy trenches, captured three prisoners and returned without any casualties or Omelet. The prisoners belonged to the 2nd Batt. 388 Landwehr Regt. and form	

Army Form C. 2118.

16 Welch Regt

(4)

WAR DIARY
or
INTELLIGENCE SUMMARY.
(Erase heading not required.)

Place	Date	Hour	Summary of Events and Information	Remarks and references to Appendices
BOESINGHE	1917 June 6		useful information was obtained from them. The right party under 2Lt J.O.Jones was unfortunately not so successful – on entering the trench the party encountered a group of the enemy and a stiff fight ensued in which the leader of the party is reported to have been killed, and Six other ranks wounded. (True Seniority) The majority, if not all of the enemy must have been accounted for as the party were able to return, carrying the wounded, without further casualties. The body of 2Lt J.O.Jones was unfortunately not recovered. He said, though a comparatively small one, strotenato, as during the six hundreds that this sector has been held by the division, many attempts have been made to cross the Canal without success by the and other units. The enemy heavily shelled BOESINGHE with 10cm between 3.0 – 4.0 am to 5.50 a. gun and 10.5cm Hows, and again intermittently throughout the day, and The front area was shelled intermittently throughout the day, and retaliation was asked for on several occasion, but was not very effective, though accidents amounts are faint – Casualties:- Officers killed 1. 2Lt J.O.Jones Wounded 1. 2Lt T.Blanco. O.R. wounded 9.	

Army Form C. 2118.

Welsh. Regt.

WAR DIARY
or
INTELLIGENCE SUMMARY.
(Erase heading not required.)

Place	Date	Hour	Summary of Events and Information	Remarks and references to Appendices
BOESINGHE	1917 June 6		Relief relieved by 11 S.W.B. in front line and in relief moved to Stuffort area. Relief complete 11.30 p.m. Disposition Bn Hqrs BLEUET Farm B&C Coys - left and right Coys X line A Coy MARIE JEANNE Fm D Coy PARADOU Fm	Appendix I
	" 7		Day spent in cleaning up. Heard nothing particular by night - Quiet day - occasional light shells on X line. About 10.45 p.m enemy fired a number of 77mm gas shells on Rte ELVERDINGHE–BOESINGHE road and around ELVERDINGHE. Some effects of the gas were felt for about five minutes, when all ranks put on their respirators, but it quickly cleared as there was a fairly fresh wind. Casualties. O.R wounded 2.	
	" 8		Extract from D.R.O. 2084 - Rewards for Services in the field dated 3rd June 1917 The Distinguished Service Order - Lieut Col F.W. Smith The Welsh Regt. Bar to granted Conduct Medal - 238884 R.S.M Clifford Lewis " "X" line heavily shelled about 2.30–3.0 am – otherwise a fairly quiet day. Usual working parties. Casualties Nil.	

Army Form C. 2118.

16 Welch Regt.

(6)

WAR DIARY
or
INTELLIGENCE SUMMARY.
(Erase heading not required.)

Instructions regarding War Diaries and Intelligence Summaries are contained in F.S. Regs., Part II. and the Staff Manual respectively. Title pages will be prepared in manuscript.

Place	Date	Hour	Summary of Events and Information	Remarks and references to Appendices
BOESINGHE SECTION	1917 June 9		A fairly quiet day. usual intermittent shelling of roads, communication trenches &c at night. Normal working parties. Casualties OR Wounded 2.	
	" 10		X Line heavily shelled between 3.30 - 3.50 a.m. Usual intermittent shelling commenced at night — normal working parties. Casualties Nil	
	" 11		X Line heavily shelled between 2.45 - 3.30 a.m. and not occasional light shells during the day. A few rounds Whizbang burst nr EMILE Fm during the afternoon — Usual working parties formed. Road &c shelled intermittently at night — Casualties OR wounded 1.	
	" 12		X Line shelled between 3.15 - 4.40 am and again 11.0 - 4.30 pm with 4pn. Batt. Relieved by 17 R.W.F. relief complete 11.30 pm. Intermittent shelling of roads &c during the night. Casualties Nil	Appendix II
	" 13		On relief by 17 R.W.F. the Batt. moved to "A" Reserve Area (ROUSSELL Fm and ELVERDINGHE) disposition — Bn Hqrs. and B + C Coys ROUSSELL Fm, A + D Coy in ELVERDINGHE DEFENCES — Day spent in resting — Normal working parties at	

2353 Wt. W2511/1454 700,000 5/15 D, D. & L. A.D.S.S./Forms/C. 2118.

Army Form C. 2118.

16 Welch Regt.

WAR DIARY
or
INTELLIGENCE SUMMARY.
(Erase heading not required.)

Ref. Sheets 28 & 27 –

Place	Date	Hour	Summary of Events and Information	Remarks and references to Appendices
ELVERDINGHE	1917 June 13		night. "D" Company burying Cable in LANCASHIRE F.M. Section. Casualties Nil	
	" 14		A quiet day – Inspection parade under Coy officers. Wood working parties, "B" Coy burying Cable in LANCASHIRE F.M. Section. Latter party were heavily shelled, and the work much interfered with. Casualties O.R. Wounded 2.	
	" 15		A quiet day. Some shelling of Battery position near WELSH F.M. The Balln. was relieved by the 3rd Bn. Grenadier Guards and on completion of relief (7.30 pm) moved to PROVEN – Central Camp – Casualties Nil	Appendix III
			A Coy and 24268 L/Cpl D.J. Collins awarded Military Medal awarded to 23961 Cpl. W.E. Richards, 23003 Cpl. T.B. Tobiasen, 110910 Pte R. Pugh. 23539 Pte W. Johnson "B" Coy – for gallantry in action in connection with the raid on night June 5/6. 1917.	
PROVEN	" 16		During the morning : general cleaning up and inspection parade under Company Arrangements "[illegible]" Battalion parade at 2.30 pm and inspected by the Commanding Officer – Casualties Nil –	

Army Form C. 2118.

WAR DIARY
or
INTELLIGENCE SUMMARY.
(Erase heading not required.)

16th Welch Regt.

Ref. BELGIUM Sheet 27 & 28

Place	Date	Hour	Summary of Events and Information	Remarks and references to Appendices
PROVEN	1917 June 17		Lt.Col. F.N. Smith. DSO. returned from leave & absence to U.K. and resumed command of the batt. Major JR Angus resuming duties as second in command. Church parade on camp parade ground. C of E 9 a.m. Non Conformist 10 a.m. At the conclusion of the C of E Service the G.O.C. 115 Inf Bde. presented military medal Ribbon & also to named NCO's & men, also to Cpl. Jay, 115 TMB and the Ribbon of the Croix de Guerre (French) to 23086 Sgt. D. Williams of this batt. Casualties Nil	
	" 18		Battalion parade for inspection by Commanding Officer, 9.0 a.m. – Remainder of the day resting – at 9.0 p.m. the batt. left PROVEN by train for trek in the CANAL BANK. Bn. Hqrs. remained at PROVEN. Casualties Nil	Appendix IV
	" 19		Working parties therefrom near CANAL BANK mobilised intermittently throughout the day, also when returning, on the roads near ELVERDINGHE. Batt. returned, entraining at ELVERDINGHE at 3.30 a.m. arrived in PROVEN 5.15 a.m. Day spent cleaning up & resting.	
	" 20		Entrained at 9.0 p.m. and returned to CANAL BANK & take over. Casualties O.R. Wounded 5 (19/6)	Appendix V

WAR DIARY or INTELLIGENCE SUMMARY

Army Form C. 2118.

16th Welch Regt

Place	Date	Hour	Summary of Events and Information	Remarks and references to Appendices
PROVEN	1917 June 21		Working parties and bivouac near CANAL BANK shelled considerably during the day. Casualties O.R. wounded 4.	Ref BELGIUM Sheets 27 & 28
	22		Battn returned to PROVEN by train from ELVERDINGHE arriving at 5:30 am having been delayed by a breakdown on the railroad. Casualties Nil	
			Day spent in resting -	
	23		Battalion parade, inspection by Commanding Officer and parade. Holiday. C.O. arrangements - Major J. Lloyd assumes duties Second in Command vice Major J. Injen in afternoon 6.ht. 2nd AD. Jones of the Batln awarded the Military Cross - he led one of the working parties across the Canal on night June 5/6th. Casualties Nil	
	24		Battn proceeded by train from PROVEN for working parties on CANAL BANK - Commander shelling of the Battn at work on the CANAL BANK - Casualties OR. 16 or 17 wounds 2 wounds S. area throughout the day. Casualties.	Appendix VI
	25		Battn bivouacked for the night in the vicinity of RIVOLI F.M. and continued work on CANAL BANK - Casualties wounded OR 1 other 1st F.Coy RE Returned by train from ELVERDINGHE arriving at PROVEN about 12 midnight -	

WAR DIARY
or
INTELLIGENCE SUMMARY.
(Erase heading not required.)

Army Form C. 2118.

Mouter Ref. Sheet 5A-1:100,000

Place	Date	Hour	Summary of Events and Information	Remarks and references to Appendices
PROVEN	1917 June 26		Day spent in Resting and preparing for move. Battn. paraded for inspection by Commanding Officer at 4.0 p.m. Battn. moved to CAESTRE area by motor lorries leaving PROVEN	
CAESTRE	" 27	12.30 p.m. 9.0 a.m.	arrived Casualties Nil. Battn. moved to FEBVIN-PALFART - (ST HILAIRE AREA) by motor lorry	Appendix VII
FEBVIN-PALFART	" 28	at 9.0 a.m. 12 noon.	leaving CAESTRE arrived FEBVIN PALFART 12 noon. Battalion billetted in Barns etc.	
	" 29		Training under Battalion arrangements.	
	" 30		Training under Battn. arrangements - Inter platoon football trny etc. had to be cancelled owing to wet weather in the afternoon.	

J.M.Smith
Lt. Col.
Comdg. 16 Bn. Welsh Regt.

WAR DIARY or INTELLIGENCE SUMMARY

Army Form C. 2118.

115/38 Vol 20

Hazebrouck (Belgium)

Ref. Sheet 5A 1:100,000

Place	Date	Hour	Summary of Events and Information	Remarks and references to Appendices
FEBVIN-PALFART	1917 July 1		Battalion in 1st Army Training Area – Disposition – Bn. Hqrs. and H. Coys. with Transport lines – FEBVIN-PALFART. Billeted – Read Church parade.	
	2		Training under Battalion arrangement at FEBVIN-PALFART.	
	3		Do	
	4		Do	
	5		Do	
	6		Training under Brigade arrangements – Practise attack over training area – EQUINGATTE –	
	7		Do	
	8		Read Church parade.	
	9		Training under Battalion arrangements FEBVIN-PALFART.	
	10		Training under Brigade arrangements – Cuthwaite pattach over training area	
	11		Training under Battalion arrangements. FEBVIN-PALFART.	
	12		Training under Divisional arrangements in manoeuvre area – Practise attack.	Appendix I

Army Form C. 2118.

WAR DIARY
or
INTELLIGENCE SUMMARY.
(Erase heading not required.)

16 Bn Welch Regt.

Ref. THEROUANNE Maps 1/40,000

Place	Date	Hour	Summary of Events and Information	Remarks and references to Appendices
FERMIN-PALFART	1917 July 13		The Battn., having bivouacked for the night - carried out night operations and returned to billets -	
	" 14		Very wet - "A" Coy carried out field firing practice on range at R30c18. Lt.Col Antsmith DSO 16 Welch Regt acting Brigade Commander. Major J.A. Angus assumed command of the Battalion	
	" 15		Voluntary Church Parade.	
	" 16		Brigade commenced march to forward area - Battn moved off at 7.0 a.m by march route to GUARBECQUE - Billeted.	Appendix II
GUARBECQUE	" 17		Battn proceeded to CAESTRE area - Camp at V11d82 (Sheet 27) - by march route	III
CAESTRE	" 18		Battn moved to EECKE area, Headquarters P24a65 (Sheet 27) - by march route	
EECKE	" 19		Battn moved by march route to Camp near PROVEN - Appro E16a84 (Sheet 27)	
PROVEN	" 20		Inspection parade under Company arrangements. Lieut Col Fox Smith resumed Command of the Battn.	
Near St SIXTE	" 21		Battn moved to the Corps Staging area - K STROUD Camp -	Appendix IV
	" 22		Usual Church Parades - "B" Coy proceeded to "X" Line - Major MILLS F.D. Knebworth	
	" 23		Battalion training and reorganization for operations - the assembly trenches -	

Army Form C. 2118.

16 Welch Regt.

WAR DIARY
or
INTELLIGENCE SUMMARY.
(Erase heading not required.)

Place	Date	Hour	Summary of Events and Information	Remarks and references to Appendices
Near ST. SIXTE	1917 July 24		Battalion training and reorganization for operations. 'B' Coy. in "X Hut" heavily shelled with gas shell. Suffered a number of casualties. Casualties - Officer wounded (gas) 2/Lt C.J. PICTON. O.R. wounded 1, wounded (gas) 15.	Ref. Sheet 27 + 28
	25		Battalion training & reorganization — Casualties wounded O.R. 4.	
	26		do — do	
	27		do — do	
	28		do — Casualties wounded O.R. 4.	
	29		Usual Church parade. Battalion (less Reserve details proceeded to CORPS REST CAMP - HERZEELE near Major J.C. Lloyd) moved by track 9 to VOX VRIE Fm	
	30		Battalion less first reserve details and administrative staff moved to assembly trenches in B.22.a & 16.s (Sheet 28 NW) leaving VOX VRIE Fm at 8.45 pm. A Coy attached as Divisional Carrying party, D Coy (less 1 platoon) detached in maintenance of tracks.	
	31		For details of action (See war diary for August)	

F.M. Smith
Lt Col.
Comdg 16th Bn Welch Regt

WAR DIARY or INTELLIGENCE SUMMARY

Army Form C. 2118.

16 Bn WELCH REGT

Vol 21

Place	Date	Hour	Summary of Events and Information	Remarks and references to Appendices
PILCKEM	1917 July 30 to Aug 5		Battalion in action – See Operation Order No.143 etc and narrative attached	Appendix I
	" 6		On relief moved out to ELVERDINGHE CHATEAU where the Battalion rested	" II
			to evening, breakfasted by Train at 9.30 p.m. to INTERNATIONAL CORNER, Reczas to ST SIXTE CAMP.	
ST SIXTE	" 7		Day spent cleaning and refitting	
	" 8		Cleaning and inspection of Arms Hd inspected by Gen in Btd at Bn Hdqrs. Reorganization and Training	
	" 9		do	
	" 10		do	
	" 11		do	
	" 12		Minor Changes in cadres – G.O.C. M'Rie attended services of 14th & 11th Div in Bn Hdqrs detail. – Reorganizing and Training	
	" 13		do	
	" 14		do	
	" 15		holding school in addition to Bgde Lewis Gunners. 23402 Pte JONES W (Late of transport) and 50111 Pte REES W had narrow attacks on Bgde Bayonet School having to evacuate	

WAR DIARY or INTELLIGENCE SUMMARY

Army Form C. 2118.

(Warwick Regt.)

Place	Date	Hour	Summary of Events and Information	Remarks and references to Appendices
ST SIXTE	1917 Aug 16		Training & programme – Major H.P. Harrison returned to the Battalion today. Military medal awarded to 235597 L/Cpl BEDLEY G. (France) 51244 Pte FORDHAM R.W. and 3329 Pte BUCKLEY J. (Hartshill battle)	Ref 25 NW
	17		Training as per programme – preparations for move.	
	18		Bn. Hd. (less Hq. machine) marched & entrained. Transport & mechanical transport entrained too, in	
ELVERDINGHE			Rued to Aaronouts's CANAL BANK Reference – BATH HSES Area CANAL BANK C13 B38 – "A" & "D" Coys Eastern bank 3 Coys WEST CANAL BANK – Bn north of Br 6A. L – BOESINGHE	
	19		Quiet day. Some shelling of CANAL BANK during the night. Shells killed 2 OR –	
	20		Quiet day – Considerable gas shelling during the night – suspected 2 ORs slightly gassed	
	21		Lieut & Qr Mr to trench home Capt McFoster & Capt EE KING (A&& 11th Res Regt) and Capt McFoster awarded MILITARY CROSS	
ELVERDINGHE	22		Quiet day Battalion moved to Reformed Area.	
	23		Helen Regt Batt Hqrs CANDLE TR C8 B 37. Intermittent shelling during the day – Chiefly on/with cancelled ford corners	Appendix II

Army Form C. 2118.

WAR DIARY
or
INTELLIGENCE SUMMARY.
(Erase heading not required.)

16th Bn. Welch Regt.

Instructions regarding War Diaries and Intelligence Summaries are contained in F.S. Regs., Part II. and the Staff Manual respectively. Title pages will be prepared in manuscript.

Place	Date	Hour	Summary of Events and Information	Remarks and references to Appendices
PICKEM	August 24		Intermittent shelling chiefly on roads & batteries by day & night	
	25		Quiet day. Some gas shelling at night	
	26		Quiet day. Relieved by 11th R.W.F. and moved forward towards	Appendix IV
			position Sh. 20. N.7. Enemy heavy guns all night	
	27		Details & situation to remain stated	V
	28			
CANAL BANK	29		S.M. reached CANAL BANK about midnight 28/29th Were L.P. for move to BRUSSEL	
			ready — the men were afterwards conveyed in huts lorries	
			FARM. day spent resting	
	30		Cleaning and reorganization.	
	31		Cleaning and reorganization. inspection parade	

[signature]
Lt. Col.
Comdg. 16 Bn. Welch Regt.

WAR DIARY
or
INTELLIGENCE SUMMARY.
(Erase heading not required.)

Army Form C. 2118.

1/6 Violet Regt. Vol 22

Place	Date	Hour	Summary of Events and Information	Remarks and references to Appendices
ELVERDINGHE	1917 Sept 1		Inspection parade by G.O.C 118th Inf. Brigade at noon.	
	2		Usual Church Parade.	
	3		Reorganization and Training. G.O.C 118 Inf Bde presented Medal Ribbons to Bn.	
	4		Bn TESTELEM. Aid. and to Serjt F. Edwards. Hope Reati & Ptes. Dane, Forshaw and Buckley.	Appendix I
			Bn. relieved 1/4 R Welsh Regt. in reserve CANAL BANK.	
	5		9:50 pm Hostile bombs from enemy aeroplanes dropped in vicinity	
			Three days normal work of parties provided for salvage and carrying.	
			Few light HE. shells fell near bivouac about 10o.p. pm. day 4 or	2
	6		Quiet day - Coys not on working parties Training and firing on ranges.	
	7		Quiet day - Working parties and Training during day - to night	
			Capt F. V. BRACHER Lt. M.G BOSTOCK & 2/Lt F.W.MOORSOM while reconnoitering to Bevoir & area between IRON CROSS and STEENBEEK were bombed.	
			night the latter was injured in right arm. Capt Bracker being N. Stevenson the assistant step. officer to hospital being wounded 3oR.	
	8		Quiet day - usual working parties and Training.	
	9		Relieved by 1/2 Br Regt. & on relief moved by Bus and hand routes to bivouac area PROVEN.	Appendix II

WAR DIARY or INTELLIGENCE SUMMARY.

Army Form C. 2118.

Place	Date	Hour	Summary of Events and Information	Remarks and references to Appendices
Proven	1917 Sep/1/16	11 a.m	Cleaning and reorganization	
	11		Training under Battalion arrangement. — S.O.C. 115 Brigade presented Medal ribbon to 565002 Sgt Appley, 23382 Cpl A. J. Johnson, 23969 Cpl J. Hill, 56583 L/Cpl O.B. Tanner, 23736 L/Cpl J. Whitlock.	Appendix III
	12	9 a.m	Battalion proceeded to EECKE area, by march route	" IV
EECKE	13	9 a.m	Battalion proceeded to MOREGUE area, by march route	" V
MOREGUE	14	9 a.m	Battalion proceeded to ESTAIRES area, by march route	" VI
ESTAIRES	15	9 a.m	Battalion proceeded to WATERLANDS area, by march route, less Lewis Gun Teams which proceeded to the Front line, HOUPLINES L/H Sub-sector	
WATERLANDS	16	9 a.m	Battalion proceeded to the HOUPLINES L/H Sub-sector & relieved the 4/5th L.N. Lancs. Relief completed 11.50 p.m.	Appendix VII
HOUPLINES	17		Quiet day.	
	18		Quiet day. — Major A.R. Headman assumed command of the Batt vice Lieut Col J.W. Smith D.S.O. granted leave to U.K. Period 19th to 29th September 1917. Captain W.J. Todger assumes duties as second in	

Army Form C. 2118.

WAR DIARY
or
INTELLIGENCE SUMMARY.
(Erase heading not required.)

Instructions regarding War Diaries and Intelligence Summaries are contained in F.S. Regs., Part II. and the Staff Manual respectively. Title pages will be prepared in manuscript.

Place	Date	Hour	Summary of Events and Information	Remarks and references to Appendices
HOUPLINES	1917 Sept		Command vice Major M.P. Steadman	
	19th		Quiet day. 1 Off & 10 O.R's from A. Coy went out on patrol, nothing happened.	
	20		Quiet day. 1 Off & 10 O.R's from C. Coy went out on patrol, nothing happened.	
	21st		Quiet day. 2 Off & 10 O.R's from D. Coy went out on patrol, nothing happened.	
	22nd		The undermentioned are awarded the Military Medal 24070 Pte E. Zohrab, 60545 Pte J. Wharton. 32514 N.T. Conway, 60544 Pte E.A. Thompson, 54314 N.W. Jenks. 23270 Pte L. O'Shea.	Appendix VIII
			Quiet day, nothing unusual to report 1 Off & 10 O.R's from C. Coy went out on patrol, nothing happened.	
	23rd	11.17	Quiet day. Relieved by the R.W.F. Headquarters, A & B. Coys proceeded to Armentieres. D & C. Coy to Subsidiary Line.	
		12.45 24/9/17	Relief completed	
	24th		A & B Coy in the Jute Factory Armentieres. General cleaning. Working party supplied for cable burying.	
	25th		Bathing. A and B Coys training on Brigade Training ground at Erquinghem D Coy relieved in the subsidiary line in order to bathe. Working	

Army Form C. 2118.

WAR DIARY
or
INTELLIGENCE SUMMARY.
(Erase heading not required.)

Instructions regarding War Diaries and Intelligence Summaries are contained in F. S. Regs., Part II. and the Staff Manual respectively. Title pages will be prepared in manuscript.

Place	Date	Hour	Summary of Events and Information	Remarks and references to Appendices
Armentieres	Sept 25th		Working parties from A & B Coys for Cable burying and Work on Duck Avenue. C & D Coys in Subsidiary Line. Wiring parties supplied to 19th RW?	
	26th		Training under Batn arrangements on Brigade training-ground. Erquinghem	
	27th		Training under Batn arrangements. Evening A & B Coys held a Concert in the Jute Factory vacated by the 10th Hood.	
	28th		Training under Batn arrangements. 2nd Lt C J Picton assumes Command of B Coy vice Lt D B Lloyd to hospital. Working parties supplied.	
	29th		Training. Boxing contests in the evening between boxers of A and B Coys. Sketch by hand. Working parties supplied.	
	30th		Training and cleaning. A & B Coys searching the country for spies suspected to have come over in an observation balloon. Final of boxing contest A & B Coys. Capt A Meggitt leaves for Brigade school.	

Sgt Mortham Lt?
O C 10th Bn. Batn.
THE WELSH REGIMENT
(CARDIFF CITY)

WAR DIARY or INTELLIGENCE SUMMARY

Army Form C. 2118.

Place	Date	Hour	Summary of Events and Information	Remarks and references to Appendices
(October)	1st/Oct		Capt Hoggett, Lost Lyetham assume command of the Machine Gun	
			the Battalion relieved the 17th R.W.F. in the Bouzlers sub-sector.	
			The night 1/2nd Relief completed 1.10 am 2nd	Appendix 1.
	2nd		Officers and NCOs of the 5th (Provisional) Bde C.E? reconnoitre the	
			sector. Major H.P. Hickman assumes Command of the Battalion, Capt Lyttelton	
			M.C. 2nd in Command. Lieut George Thomas relinquishes Command of D	
			Coy vice Capt R.A. Hutchings.	
	3rd		Battalion in the line. Disposition as follows: A Coy Left (Goodwood)	
			D Coy Centre (Pippin) B Coy Right (Castle Park). Enemy active with	
			L and M.T.M. on Nos 4, 6, 7 posts. Patrol 10/8 noted went out to reconnoitre	
			enemy wire. Fired on a hostile wiring party.	
	4th		Battalion in the line. Enemy exceeding active during day with T.M.s	
			our artillery retaliation not sufficiently effective. During the night the	
			enemy put a heavy barrage of minnies around nos 6 and 7 Post and	
			5.9s and M.G.s on Goodwood. Busy installing our A.T.M.B. in Pip 1.	
	5th.		Battalion in the line. Artillery very active, a lot of counter battery work	

L 22

WAR DIARY
or
INTELLIGENCE SUMMARY.
(Erase heading not required.)

Army Form C. 2118.

Place	Date	Hour	Summary of Events and Information	Remarks and references to Appendices
October	5th		cont.	
"	6th		Enemy fired numerous 6.7 and 28 pdrs. Enemy H.T.M. (flying pig) registered on the enemy Battalion in the line. Our H.T.M. (flying pig) registered on the enemy F.L. and support lines. Enemy retaliation very intense especially on the left Coy's front. The 2/5. of the 17th R.W.F. relieved our Fand S line trenches.	
"	7th		Battalion relieved by the 17th R.W.F. Dispositions A and B Coys left and right subsidiary line respectively, D Coy and C menin platoon at the School and D platoon at Cambridge House, until Lille Factory.	App. 2/11.III.
"	8th		C & D Coys cleaning up. Working parties supplied.	
"	9th		Battalion bathing and training under Bath arrangements. Lt E Hoggarth assumes command of A Coy. Lt Hogm Thomas resumes duty with B Coy.	
"	10th		Battalion providing working parties for work on subsidiary line. Patrol of 20ff 24 oRs left our lines at C29c 1.8. to examine enemy wire. Capt R.M.Hutchinson assumes duties as 2nd in Command. Lt Hogm Thomas resumes command of A Coy.	
"	11th		Battalion providing working parties, bathing and morning parades. Patrol of 20ff 1tORs left our line at C29c 2.6. to examine enemy wire from C29c 4.3. to C29c 4.4. 8. and locate gaps in C29c 4.5. 8. and locate gaps.	

Army Form C. 2118.

WAR DIARY
or
INTELLIGENCE SUMMARY.
(Erase heading not required.)

Instructions regarding War Diaries and Intelligence Summaries are contained in F. S. Regs., Part II and the Staff Manual respectively. Title pages will be prepared in manuscript.

Place	Date	Hour	Summary of Events and Information	Remarks and references to Appendices
October	12th		Battalion supplying working parties for work on the Subsidiary Line, Edward and Irish avenues. L9s relieve the L.G's of the 17th RWF in the front and support lines. Heavy artillery cutting wire at C.29.a.4.2. A total of 2 Off. 10 O.R.'s left our lines to examine the gap made by the artillery at C.29.a.4.2.	App. IV.
	13th		Battalion relieves the 17th RWF in the Houplines subsector. Disposition C Coy left, A Coy Centre, D Coy right, B Coy in support.	
	14th		Battalion in the line. Quiet during the day. Patrols of 1 Off. 12 O.R.'s and 2 Off. 30 O.R.'s were sent out with the object of obtaining identification but were unsuccessful.	
	15th		Battalion in the line. Enemy artillery fairly active. Trench mortars were active in C.2ya. A patrol of 1 Off. 11 O.R.'s went out to examine wire in C.29.a.4.2. A patrol of 2 Off. 35 O.R.'s entered the enemy lines at C.29.a.4.2. An officer of the enemy and 1 man brought out as far as enemy wire, where the officer who was leading him over was wounded and the prisoner managed to escape back into his own line.	

Army Form C. 2118.

WAR DIARY
or
INTELLIGENCE SUMMARY.
(Erase heading not required.)

Instructions regarding War Diaries and Intelligence Summaries are contained in F. S. Regs., Part II. and the Staff Manual respectively. Title pages will be prepared in manuscript.

Place	Date	Hour	Summary of Events and Information	Remarks and references to Appendices
October	16th		Battalion in the line. Quiet throughout the day. A patrol of 1 Off. 1 O.R's examined the W side of CENSORS NOSE but failed to find any gaps in the wire. At 3.35 am a small enemy patrol was seen off No 5 post standing on the parapet outside the wire on the left flank of the post. Shots were fired and bombs thrown by both sides. One of our men was wounded.	
	17th		Battalion in the line. In the afternoon the enemy did a lot of Counter-battery shelling, and retaliation to our (Flying Pig) H.M. Fighting patrols were sent out but no enemy patrol or working parties encountered.	
	18th		Battalion in the line. Lewis Guns relieved by L.G's of 17th R.W.F. Enemy fired large numbers of L.T.M gas shells in the vicinity of CAMBRIDGE HOUSE. A patrol sent out from left Coy 7.30–10.30 pm. No enemy encountered Battalion less L.G's relieved in the line by 17th R.W.F. A & D Coys left Appendix V and Right Subsidiary line respectively C and B - 1 Platoon Jute Factory	Appendix V
	20th 21st		Cleaning up and inspection. Working parties supplied. A + B Coys training under Coy arrangements. Working parties under	

Army Form C. 2118.

WAR DIARY
or
INTELLIGENCE SUMMARY.
(Erase heading not required.)

Instructions regarding War Diaries and Intelligence Summaries are contained in F. S. Regs., Part II. and the Staff Manual respectively. Title pages will be prepared in manuscript.

Place	Date	Hour	Summary of Events and Information	Remarks and references to Appendices
O.A.	1st		under Coy arrangements. RE supervision	
	2nd		A & B Coys firing practice on 300x range at Enguinlen. Working parties supplied. Concert given by B Coy and band	
	3rd		A & B Coys bathing and training under Coy arrangements. Working parties under RE supervision	
	4th		C & D Coys bathing. A & B Coys training under Coy arrangements. Working parties supplied. Evening Concert given by A Coy and the band. 2 men relieved 2/4 of 17th RWF in the line	
	24th			
	25th		The Battalion relieves the 17th RWF in the line. Two fighting patrols out from 4 pm to 10 pm. No enemy encountered	Appendix VI.
	26th		Battalion in the line. Quiet during the day, a few to 5cm how and HTM on right Coy support and front lines	
	27th		Battalion in the line. Enemy Artillery and TM's active throughout the day. A few gas shells fired into Hougline. Two patrols of 1 off 110R each patrolled NML and examined enemy wire. No enemy patrol encountered	

Army Form C. 2118.

WAR DIARY
or
INTELLIGENCE SUMMARY.
(Erase heading not required.)

Place	Date	Hour	Summary of Events and Information	Remarks and references to Appendices
Ref.	28th		Battalion in the line. Enemy artillery and T.M's active throughout the day. Front and support lines bombarded throughout the day with 77mm and H.V's. Front and support line left Coy heavily shelled with MTM and HTM's between 11 - 11.30 am and 3pm to 4pm. At 9.30pm supported and covered by artillery and M.Gns we projected a Stokes Gas Barrage into enemy lines.	Appendix VII
	29th		Battalion in the line. At 4 am an enemy retaliated to our gas bombardment with a very heavy barrage on the left Coy HQ and No 6 and 7 posts. Enemy Artillery quiet during the day. During the afternoon the left Coy front was shelled with LTM, MTM and a few HTM's. Our Artillery doing counter battery work during afternoon. Our T.M's very active as the line.	Appendix VIII
	30th		Battalion in the line. Our R.G's relieved by the R.G's of the 17th R.In.F. Artillery quiet during the day. A patrol of 1 Off. & 8 O.R.s left our lines at C.23.b.15½ and encountered an enemy patrol of over 40. We fired on them and they hurriedly retired to their own lines.	
	31st		Battalion relieved by 17th R.In.F. On disposing A Coy left O.B.L. line to C Coy right. Appendix IX subsidiary line. Comd'g Coy's to factory. 4th Batt. C.E.F. attached for training.	Appendix IX

J.R. McAlveen Major
Comd'g 1st Batt. R.G.

A.D.S.S. Forms/C. 2118.

16 Welch Regt

WAR DIARY
or
INTELLIGENCE SUMMARY.

Place	Date	Hour	Summary of Events and Information	Remarks and references to Appendices
Armentieres	Nov 1st	Subsector	C & D Coy bathing and inspections by C.O. A & B Coy subsidiary line working under R.E. supervision. Working parties supplied.	
"	2nd		C and D Coys training under Coy arrangements. Working parties supplied for work in Armentieres and the front line. A & B Coy subsidiary line working parties.	
"	3rd		C & D Coy training under Coy arrangements. A dress team from C & D Coys and transport played and beat the 10th R.W.B. at Erquinham. Concert given by C Coy assisted by the Band. A & B Coy working parties under R.E. supervision.	
	4th		C & D Coy training under Coy arrangements. Working parties supplied. Concert given by S Companies by the Band. A & B Coy providing working and carrying parties in the line.	
	5th		C & D Coy training under Coy arrangements. Working parties supplied all day. Buses relieve the R.B's of the 17th Rnt in the line.	12/2/85
	6th		The Battalion relieves the 17th R.W.F. in the line; disposition A Coy left, C Coy centre, B Coy right, D Coy support.	Appendix 1

WAR DIARY
or
INTELLIGENCE SUMMARY.
(Erase heading not required.)

Army Form C. 2118.

Place	Date	Hour	Summary of Events and Information	Remarks and references to Appendices
Houplines Sub-sector 1101.	7th.		Battalion in the line. Artillery and T.M's fairly quiet during the day. T.M's active from 1-30 am - 3.30 am 7/8th. A patrol of 1 Off 11 OR's examined enemy wire from C 23 c Y.P. to C 23 a Y.i.1. A body of a German found in C 23 c 20.15. Identification secured.	
	8th.		Battalion in the line. Enemy Artillery and T.M's very active during the day mostly on left Coy's front. A patrol of 1 Off 11 OR's left our line at C 23 c Y.i.7. to engage any hostile patrols.	
	9th.		Battalion in the line. Enemy Artillery and T.M's fairly active throughout the day. Our Artillery fired in retaliation to enemy shelling. Two patrols of 1 Off 11 OR's each left our lines to engage any hostile patrol. An enemy patrol near C 29 a J.4. fired on	
	10th.		Battalion relieved by the 17th R.W.F. in the line. Our disposition A + B Coys left and right Subsidiary line Coy Houplines entrants, C + D Coys left and right Subsidiary line Coy Epinette Sub. sector.	Appendix ii
	11th		Battalion in the Subsidiary line under the 176th Inf. Bde and 101 S.W.B. Working parties as per programme under R.E. supervision.	

Army Form C. 2118.

WAR DIARY
or
INTELLIGENCE SUMMARY.
(Erase heading not required.)

Place	Date	Hour	Summary of Events and Information	Remarks and references to Appendices
Nov.	12th		Battalion in the Subsidiary Line. Working parties under R.E. supervision. Hostile Artillery and T.M's active during the day. Subsidiary line shelled with gas at intervals during the night.	
	13th		Battalion in the Subsidiary line. Working parties supplied for all Coys. for work on Subsid. line. Increased activity of Enemy T.M's	
	14th		Battalion in the Subsidiary line. Working parties supplied. Enemy T.M's and Artillery very active during the day. Increase in aeroplane activity on both sides. Battalion shelled with gas shells at intervals during the night.	
	15th		Battalion in the Subsidiary line. Working parties supplied. Slight decrease of hostile shelling and T.M's. In the morning our Artillery obtained fire on an S.O.S. call supposed to have been sent through by an enemy towerpigeon	
	16th		Battalion in the Left and Right sectors Subsidiary Line relieved by the 1/4 S.W.B. The Battalion relieved the 1/4 G.W.R in the Hazefore trenches.	Appendix III
	17th		Battalion in the Line. Dispositions left C Coy Centre D Coy Right B Coy Support Coy A Coy. Enemy Artillery registered on ESMEAS and CAMARIS SE Ayes and around no 5 post. Enemy T.M active during the afternoon. Very quiet night. A fighting patrol of 1 Off. cont.	

WAR DIARY
or
INTELLIGENCE SUMMARY.
(Erase heading not required.)

Army Form C. 2118.

Place	Date	Hour	Summary of Events and Information	Remarks and references to Appendices
Nev.	17th		10ff 11 O.R's left our line at C.23.c.1.3. to lie in wait for any enemy patrols. None encountered.	
	18th		Battalion in the line. Enemy Artillery and T.M's very active throughout the day. Our Battery and TRESTAGE DUMP shelled with gas shell. A patrol of 1 Off 10 O.R's left our line at C.23.a.1.6. to engage any enemy patrol. None encountered. At 5.15 pm Red lights were fired in the enemy front line extending from opposite to just down S.P's action followed.	
	19th		Battalion in the line. Enemy extremely active throughout the day, both Artillery and T.M's. Between 10 a.m and 11 a.m a very heavy barrage was put down on the whole Battn front, most intense around the spot. A fighting patrol of 1 Off 11 O.R's left our line at C.17.c.4.5. to patrol N.M.L. No enemy patrol encountered.	
	20th		Battalion in the line. A slight decrease of Enemy Artillery and T.M fire. During the morning 3 tracer shells were fired (77 mm) toward CAMBRIDGE Two of them ricochetted and went on toward Houplines. Two patrols of 1 Off 12 O.R's and 1 Off 10 O.R's left 29.c.1.7 and C.17.c.6.1.6 to engage any enemy patrol. None encountered.	

WAR DIARY or INTELLIGENCE SUMMARY

Army Form C. 2118.

Place	Date	Hour	Summary of Events and Information	Remarks and references to Appendices
Nov	21st		Battalion in the line. There was a decrease of hostile artillery fire during the day but a great increase of T.M. fire. Our Artillery/retaliation good but along the line coming. Two patrols of 2 off 10 O.R's and 1 off 100 R's left our line but engaged hostile patrol none encountered. Very quiet night	
	22nd		Battalion relieved by the 17th Regt in the line Enemy T.M's started firing very heavily at 9 am and at intervals during the day but our artillery got on to them fairly quickly and neutralised them. Batt'n proceed. to Laundry A & B Coys at the Brigade School C & D Coys. in Laundry at S	Appendix IV
	23rd		[illegible]	
	24th		[illegible]	
	25th		[illegible]	
	26th		[illegible]	

WAR DIARY
or
INTELLIGENCE SUMMARY.

Army Form C. 2118.

Place	Date	Hour	Summary of Events and Information	Remarks and references to Appendices
	Nov 9th		My artillery continues working to cut wire and cut Coy opposite a and m. A,B Coys. Holding with usual forms of working parties in the line	
	Nov 10th		Relieved during the night 11th by the line Borderers Mby 1/2 B Coy and D Coy light C Coy dispersal. Enemy Tm/m and Artillery fairly quiet during the day. Enemy very lively. Battle of Kut left Line at 2.25 15.10 the patrol NML and engaged into the Battn HQ. day quiet at night a patrol of 10K.R.R. left line front of the line & fire of 10 K.R.R. left on our front but later NM on left and engaged by Rwels gets in the line in the tree. Our Artillery carried out a distraction of rivers dwry to-day quiet but the various local operations the night left patrol NM myself out and engaged my Rwels gets in no mans.	Appendix Y

H.P. MacMiken Major
O.C. 16th Welsh Regt

Sheet 5 16/Welsh Regt

December 1917

WAR DIARY
or
INTELLIGENCE SUMMARY
Army Form C. 2118.

Place	Date	Hour	Summary of Events and Information	Remarks and references to Appendices
ARMENTIÈRES			HOUPLINES SUB-SECTOR.	
	December 1		Battalion in the line. Dispositions D. Coy right C Coy Centre A Coy left B Coy Support. Enemy Artillery quiet during day and night. Slight T.M activity on Centre Coy front during the day. A patrol of 1 off. 12 O.R.s patrolled NML without encountering any enemy patrol.	
	" 2.		Battalion in the line. During the day the enemy slightly shelled Nos 5 post, WESSEX AVE, FRYPAN and Bn HQ. Slight T.M activity on Centre Coy front. Fighting patrols out during the night.	
	" 3		Battalion in the line. Slight Artillery and T.M activity on Battn front. Fighting patrols out during night. No hostile patrols seen. Relief of Battalion (Res) Guards Div by 4th Div by 4 SR opposite Battn front.	App 1
	4.		Battalion relieved by the 17th R.W.F.	
	5.		Battalion in the subsidiary line. Dispositions L'Épinette subsector right B Coy, Left A Coy. Houplines subsector right C Coy Left D Coy.	9/24
	6.		Batt. in the Subsidiary line. Working parties supplied as per Brigade Working party table	
	7.		Battalion in the subsidiary line. Working parties as per programme.	

Sheet II   1st Welch Regt.

Army Form C. 2118.

WAR DIARY
or
INTELLIGENCE SUMMARY.
(Erase heading not required.)

Place	Date	Hour	Summary of Events and Information	Remarks and references to Appendices
Dec.	8.		Battalion in the Subsidiary line. Working parties as per programme. Artillery and Hostile TM quiet during night.	
	9		Battalion in the Subsidiary line. Working parties as per bde programme. Right Artillery shelling of Right Subsidiary Coy H.Q. Hopeline subsector.	
	10.		Battalion in the Subsidiary line. Day working parties supplied. Quiet during the day. Battalion relieved in the Subsidiary line by the 10th S.W. Bn. Battalion in Q.Gn relieve (7th Div) in the line.	Apper. 11
	11.		Battalion in the line. Dispositions C Coy (Right) A Coy (Centre) D Coy (Left) B Coy support. 2/Lts relieved at dawn. Hostile Artillery and TM quiet.	
	12.		Battalion in the line. Enemy Artillery quiet. TM fairly active. A battery during the day. A patrol of 1 off 11 O.R.s examined enemy wire in Coy CH.28 e H. Battalion in the line. Enemy Artillery informed. A fighting patrol left our	
	13.		O/B MTM located and Artillery informed. A fighting patrol left our lines and patrolled NML without encountering any hostile patrols.	
	13.		Battalion in the line. Hostile Artillery and LTM shelled the left Coy front at intervals during the day and night.	13/12/Ct Appx 12
	14.		Battalion in the line. Lt Col. Fox Smith assumes Command of the Battn.	13/12/Ct Appx 13

Army Form C. 2118.

Sheet III   10/11/24/a/b/c/d/e/f

WAR DIARY
or
INTELLIGENCE SUMMARY.
(Erase heading not required.)

Instructions regarding War Diaries and Intelligence Summaries are contained in F. S. Regs., Part II. and the Staff Manual respectively. Title pages will be prepared in manuscript.

Place	Date	Hour	Summary of Events and Information	Remarks and references to Appendices
Vieille Chapelle	14		vice Maj A.A. Andrews. Slight increase of Hostile Artillery and T.M. fire.	
	15.		Battn in the line. Considerable decrease of Enemy Artillery and T.M. fire. Night exceptionally quiet. A patrol of 1 Off. 1 O.R. & 10 O.R. & 1 our lines to examine enemy wire and engage any hostile patrol, have encountered.	
	do.		Battn in the line relieved by the 19th Bn. 3. Very slight Artillery and T.M. activity during the day.	App III
	17.		Battalion in the LAUNDRY Erquinghem Rd. Cleaning and bathing parade.	
	18.		Battalion in the LAUNDRY. C.O. inspect billets. Training under Coy arrangements.	
	19.		Battalion relieved by the 34th Battn A.I.F. Battn embussed under Maj W.C. Foster at Erquinghem Church and proceed to WITTERNESSE.	App IV
	20.		Battn in WITTERNESSE. General cleaning up.	
	21.		do. do. Training on ground at ROMEY under Battn arrangements	
	22.		do. do. Training under Battn arrangements	App V
	23.		do. do. Training under Battn arrangements. L.G. and rifle range practice	App VI App VII

16/Welch Regt.

Sheet IV

Army Form C. 2118.

December 1917

WAR DIARY
or
INTELLIGENCE SUMMARY.
(Erase heading not required.)

Place	Date	Hour	Summary of Events and Information	Remarks and references to Appendices
WITTERNESSE	Dec. 24		Training under Batt. arrangements. Visited by G.O.C. Brigade	
	25		Christmas Day. All ranks had Turkey & Christmas Pudding. The Commanding Officer visited all Companies during Dinner	
	26		Boxing Day. Battalion bathing at Flechenelle.	
	27		Training. Batt. attack on defended wood near Romley. Attack watched by G.O.C. Brigade.	
	28		Training. Capt. H.LL. JONES rejoined Battn. after being wounded. Capt. A. MEGGITT returned from Course at ALDERSHOT, & 2/Lts TRUESLOND, VANN, R. BOVEN, R.P. BENNETT, D.G. DAVIES, & DUDLEY joined Battn. as Reinforcements.	
	29 30 31		Sunday Church Parade. Training. Bomb Throwing Day. Since Xmas Day the ground has been covered with snow, and the cold weather has made training difficult. Full use has been made of the Musketry & L.G. Ranges, and of the P.T. & B.F. Instructors lent by the XI Corps Reinforcements Camp.	E. H. Smith Lt Col

Sheet 1. January 1918 16/Welch Regt.

WAR DIARY
or
INTELLIGENCE SUMMARY.
(Erase heading not required.)

Army Form C. 2118.

Place	Date	Hour	Summary of Events and Information	Remarks and references to Appendices
WITTERNESSE map Ref: FRANCE Sheet 36A 40,000 N.13.6.	1st.		Training.	H.728
	2nd.		Route March with transport (1st Line) — ESTRÉE BLANCHE — BASSE BOULOGNE — MARTHES — BLESSY — WITTERNESSE.	
	3rd.		2/Lt. H.A.DAVIES & O.JENKINS reported their arrival — posted to C. & B. Coys respectively. They came from 19/Welch Regt, where they had been for a few days. Visit from G.O.C. 115th Inf Bde., Bde Major, G.S.O. 1 Division, & Gen. Allen U.S.A. Army this Staff. During the morning the Battalion carried out an attack in the afternoon the Generals & their Staffs watched a Coy doing Musketry in Box Respirator, firing from the hip, Physical drill, and Company drill.	H.728 H.728 I H.728
	4th.		Training. Major H.P. HERDMAN (or leave in U.K.) struck off Strength Medical Board onduck. Lieut N.F. RENSHAW arrived 1.1.18 Placew on being GE	9/25 7ditto W.728
	5th.		Draft of 50 men arrived from 19/Welch Regt (transferred) Training.	W.728 W.728
	6th.		Sunday. Church Service.	

Sheet 2.   January 1918.   16/Welch Regt.

WAR DIARY
or
INTELLIGENCE SUMMARY.
(Erase heading not required.)

Army Form C. 2118.

Place	Date JAN	Hour	Summary of Events and Information	Remarks and references to Appendices
WITTERNESSE	7th.		Battalion Outpost Scheme.	
	8th.		Battn. battle at FLECHINELLE.	
			Following Officers & N.C.O. were mentioned in dispatches. (supplement to London Gazette d/14.12.17) Lieut. Col. F.W. SMITH, D.S.O., Capt. H.L. JONES, Lieut. T.H. JOHNSON 11577m.s, Capt. H.M. SALMON V.	H.B
			32570 L. Sgt. A. GLEDHILL. Following N.C.Os awarded D.C.M. (New Years Honours Gazette d/1.1.18) 23361 C.Q.M.S. W.H. CARNIE, 23679 Pte. T. CONELL.	H.B
	9th.		Up to now the 100× and 30× Muskety Ranges also 30× decn Gun Range near LINGHEM Camp belonging to XV Corps Reinforcement had been completely at disposal of Battn. Owing to Divnl. Reinf. Wings coming to Corps, Battn. has had to give up these Ranges and Musketry now carried out in quarries at QUERNES H.P.	
	10th.		Training.	
			Capt. R.H. HUTCHINGS to XV Corps School as Instructor in Bombing & Stokes Mortar.	
			Lieut. T.G. SILLEM M.C. took over Command of "D" Coy vice Capt. R.H. HUTCHINGS.	H.B
			Lieut. W.F. RENSHAW took over Bandpt. vice Lieut. T.G. SILLEM, M.C.	H.B
	11th.		Training.	
			Snow which has been falling since 24th Decr 1917 is still several inches thick.	H.B

Sheet 3. January 1918. 16/Welch Regt.

WAR DIARY or INTELLIGENCE SUMMARY.

Army Form C. 2118.

(Erase heading not required.)

Place	Date	Hour	Summary of Events and Information	Remarks and references to Appendices
WITTERNESSE	12th		Musketry Competition (Bns. Recreational Competitions) started on 100x Range	
	13th		Sunday. Church Service.	
	14th		Musketry Comp. Finished. Result:- A Coy 1332 pts. C Coy 1223. D Coy 1034. B Coy 931. Boxing & Cross Country Running most evenings.	
	14th		Bathing at FLECHINELLE.	
	15th		Met. Training impossible out of doors. Musketry, Anti-Gas drill, in Billets.	
	16th		Lt. G. Thomas (at Base) passed B.1. & struck off strength 11.1.18.	
	16th		Sheet No hearing ctrol Joins Batts. 1st C Coy 1216. 2nd O/C Coy 169 pts 3rd A Coy 133 W.G.Cripps, E.Griffiths, W.S.H.Brace, J.E.L.Vaughan & 4th B Coy 124	
	17th		Training in area of Billets. G.O.C. Brigade & B.M. came round, also E.O.C.	
	17th		114/Bn. Orders	
	18th		Batt. left WITTERNESSE at 10 a.m. (after 30 days, the longest spell in Reserve Area since our coming to FRANCE). Reached GUARBECQ at 12.40 p.m.	
GUARBECQ (France 36A 40,000)	19th		Brigade From re-Parties to buy. Left GUARBECQ 8.45 a.m and proceeded via ST VENANT and MERVILLE to	
NEUF BERQUIN (France 36A 20,000 L.14. L.21)			NEUF BERQUIN Arrived 1.30 p.m.	
	20th		Sunday. Church Service.	
	21st		A Coy to BERGUETTE (France 36A 40,000 O.16.c.1.7.) to work for 1st Army Clearing Post.	

Sheet 1.　　January 1918.　　16/Welch Regt.

Army Form C. 2118.

WAR DIARY
or
INTELLIGENCE SUMMARY.

(Erase heading not required.)

Place	Date	Hour	Summary of Events and Information	Remarks and references to Appendices
	JANY			
NEUF BERQUIN	21st (Cont)		Major W.T. FOSTER, M.C., also to BERGUETTE as Commandant of the Depot.	H.R.S.
	22nd		"B" Coy, who have 1 Platoon at Brigade School, sent 51 ORs on Guards and Extra Regtl duties in ESTAIRES & MERVILLE. Batt. left with 2 Coys in 1st Line.	H.R.S.
	23rd		Working Parties. Training. Bathing. Brigade X Country Runs. 1st 19/R.W.F. 2nd 17/R.W.F. 3rd 16/Welch 4th 11/S.W.B. 5th 115/T.M.B.	H.R.S. H.R.S.
	24th		Working Parties. Every available man employed	H.R.S.
	25th		Working Parties. "	H.R.S.
	26th		Working Parties.	H.R.S.
	27th		Sunday. Working Parties as usual. Col. Smith went to CHOQUES for a flight with R.F.C.	H.R.S.
	28th		Working Parties. Great improvement in weather. Field and every night clean.	H.R.S.
	29th		Working Parties. Transport making great efforts for Brigade Transport Competition.	H.R.S.
	30th		Working Parties.	J.W. Smith Lt.

Sheet 5. January 1918. 16/Welch Regt.

Army Form C. 2118.

WAR DIARY
INTELLIGENCE SUMMARY.
(Erase heading not required.)

Place	Date	Hour	Summary of Events and Information	Remarks and references to Appendices
NEUF BERQUIN	Jany 31st		"A" Coy less 1 Platoon returned from BERGUETTE. They had been employed in erecting a Clearing Depôt for the 1st Army to transport of Battalions which would be disbanded under G.H.Q. Scheme for reducing all Infantry Brigades to 3 Battalions. "A" Coy had received the Depôt, & as soon as it was completed others were received to dismantle the whole Depôt. Working Parties.	

W.P.S.

E.M. Smith Lt Col

6 Sheet 1.   February 1918

16/Welch Regt (Cardiff City Batln)

Army Form C. 2118.

WAR DIARY
INTELLIGENCE SUMMARY

Place	Date	Hour	Summary of Events and Information	Remarks and references to Appendices
NEUF BERQUIN France 36 A 40,000 L.14.c.3.1.	Feby 1st		The remaining Platoon of "A" Coy. with Major W.J. FOSTER M.C. returned from BERGUETTE.	
	2nd		The Brigade Transport Competition, for which the Battalion Transport had worked so hard, took place at 11.30 a.m. It was won by this Battn. and G.O.C. Division (Major-Genl G.G. BLACKADER, C.B., D.S.O., A.D.C.), in presenting the Prize of 200 francs to the Commanding Officer, said that he had never seen finer transport in his life.	
	3rd		Instructions were received some time ago that it had been decided to reduce each Brigade to 3 Battalions. To-day written orders for the disbanding of this Battn. here received. The Transport is going away to the M.G.C. 16 Officers and 30 O.R.s are being transferred to other Battns. The remainder go to the Corps Pool.	
	4th		Working Parties on Aplee Defences. In the afternoon the Battalion paraded, the Commanding Officer explained the system of Reorganisation. He added that this Parade probably be the last Battn. Parade in the history of	

Sheet 2.

Sheet 2.   February 1918   Army Form C. 2118.

WAR DIARY
INTELLIGENCE SUMMARY.

of 16th (Cnd if Cdt) Bn. Welch Regt

(Erase heading not required.)

Instructions regarding War Diaries and Intelligence Summaries are contained in F. S. Regs., Part II. and the Staff Manual respectively. Title pages will be prepared in manuscript.

Place	Date	Hour	Summary of Events and Information	Remarks and references to Appendices
NEUF BERQUIN	Feb 4th		the Battn, and wished all Ranks success whenever they might be posted. He pointed out that the shortage of manpower was the cause of the radical changes, and although the older members of the Battn, some of whom had served in the field with the Battn for over 2 years, would feel the wrench very greatly, still he was sure everybody would continue to do his best in his new Unit.	
	5th.		At C Coys have been chosen for transfer.	
	6th.		8 Officers (mostly A Coy) & 150 O.R. of A Coy proceeded to join the 19/Welch Regt. C. 56 O.R. of B & 40 " " D & B Co 15/Welch Regt	
			The G.O.C. 115/Bde inspected the Draft before they left. The Band played the Drafts away, & everybody turned out to say good-bye. The men felt the parting very much, & the fact that on transfer the "A" & "C" "Colour Badge" always so proudly worn, would have to be taken out of the Battn. thus losing its identity, was hard to bear. It was generally felt that if the comb-out had been pretty carried out at home, it would not have been necessary to	

A6945 Wt. W1422/M1160 350,000 12/16 D. D. & L. Forms/C/2118/14.

March 3 February 1918 16th (Cardiff City) Bn Welch Rgt

Army Form C. 2118.

WAR DIARY
or
INTELLIGENCE SUMMARY.
(Erase heading not required.)

Place	Date	Hour	Summary of Events and Information	Remarks and references to Appendices
NEUF BERQUIN Bth	6th		break up a Battalion to which everybody was proud to belong. The Kingston Personnel left today to join 33/Division at	
	7th		BOISDINGHEM (Map HAZEBROUCK S¹ 10920 (B.4.) The Commanding Officer Frapp? to them before they left. The Linen, told them that, although they were being detached from the Battalion they were not losing their identity, they could still wear their badges & be allowed to do the Cardiff City badge upon, who only a few days before had proved themselves to be the truest Bandgat in the Brigade, & in the words of the G.O.C. 38/Division "the truest Battn. I have ever seen." G.O.C. Brigade met them shortly afterwards & wished them God Spe. All Battalion Stores were handed in. Baths were left with what it stands up in plus Blankets, Cutlery, Razors, Boxes & Camp kettles. Even the Camp Camp, which is the Official Identification mark of the Battalion, has been taken away. Orders received to move to WERNES on 10th to join Corps	
	8th			

Sheet 1.   February 1918.   16th (Cardiff City) Bn. Welch Regt.

Army Form C. 2118.

WAR DIARY
INTELLIGENCE SUMMARY
(Erase heading not required.)

Place	Date Feby.	Hour	Summary of Events and Information	Remarks and references to Appendices
NEUF BERQUIN	8th		Reinforcement Depot. The present strength of the Battalion is 1 Lt. Col. 5 Captains 4 Lieuts. 18 2nd Lieuts. 5 W.O's. C.Q.M. 4 C.Q.M.S. 13 Sergts. 32 L/Sgts. 8 Corpls. 25 L/Cpls. 494 Ptes. All preparations to move made.	
	9th		Move orders cancelled. Conor Stamp sent back to the Batt. The following have been awarded the Belgian "Croix de Guerre". 23881 C.S.M. GILBERT J.M. 23588 Corpl. TOWNSEND W.E. (now of 90th A.E.Cos 13 down G.P.)	
	10th		Sunday Church Parades	
	11th		Working Parties	
MENEGATE CAMP Sh. 36. Vaor. B. 12. a. 3. 2.	12th		Battalion moved to MENEGATE CAMP. Dr STEENWERCK. to work on Corps Defence extending trench instruction. Camp shared by surplus personnel (about 300) of 2/1st South Lancs. Regt. (57th Divn.) also an advance.	
	13th		Quiet day very wet.	
	14th		The whole of the Battalion employed on digging defences under the instructions of C.R.E. Reserve Division (57 Divn)	
	15th		Working Parties. The men are finishing their task by 1 p.m.	

Sheet 5 February 1918 16th (Cardiff City) Bn. Welch Regt.

Army Form C. 2118.

WAR DIARY
or
INTELLIGENCE SUMMARY.
(Erase heading not required.)

Place	Date Feby	Hour	Summary of Events and Information	Remarks and references to Appendices
LIMEINGATTE CAMP	16th		Working Parties	
	17th		Sunday. Church Paraded. Divine Service in Camp	
	18th		Working Parties.	
	19th		Working Parties	
	20th		Working Parties	
	21st		"	
	22nd		News received that the remaining personnel of this Battn is to be merged, with remains of 15/R.W.F and 10/Welch Regt, into what is to be known as No.1 Entrenching Battn. Entrenching Battns are to be formed of all disbanded battalions; these will work on the Rear Area defences, but will be available as Reinforcements. Lt. Col. F.W. SMITH is to administer Army Group of these Entrenching Battalions, with Headquarters at BRUAY. Capt & Adjt. H.L. JONES is to be Adjutant & Quartermaster of No.1 Entrenching Battalion. The personnel forming these Battalions retain their identity,	

A6945 Wt. W1442/M1160 350,000 12/16 D. D. & L. Forms/C.2118/14.

Sheet 6   February 1918   16/Welch Regt (Cardiff City Bn.)

Army Form C. 2118.

WAR DIARY
or
INTELLIGENCE SUMMARY.
(Erase heading not required.)

Instructions regarding War Diaries and Intelligence Summaries are contained in F. S. Regs., Part II. and the Staff Manual respectively. Title pages will be prepared in manuscript.

Place	Date FEBY.	Hour	Summary of Events and Information	Remarks and references to Appendices
MENEGATE CAMP	22nd		until posted away to other Battalions.	
	23rd		Lt. Col. SMITH left yesterday to take up his duties at BRUAY. Lt. Col. T.H. MORGAN, D/S.W.B. arrived to commence organisation of No. 1 Entrenching Battn, which is to have its Headquarters at MENEGATE CAMP.	
	24th		Church Services. Working Parties.	
	25th		" "	
	26th		Personnel of 19/Welch + 15/R.W.F. arrived.	
		→	16/Welch carried out working parties. Day spent in organising Battn into 4 Companies.	
	27th		Formation of No. 1 Entrenching Battn completed. A Coy consists of O/R. of 19/Welch. B Coy. 16/Welch + 19/Welch. C Coy 19/Welch. D Coy 15/R.W.F + 16/Welch. Strength of each Coy about 320. From to day the 16/Welch ceases to exist as a Battalion	

www.ingramcontent.com/pod-product-compliance
Lightning Source LLC
Chambersburg PA
CBHW081541160426
43191CB00011B/1807